Practical English Workbook

Practical English Workbook

SEVENTH EDITION

Floyd C. Watkins
Late of Emory University

William B. Dillingham
Emeritus, Emory University

John T. Hiers
Valdosta State University

Matthew G. Hearn
Valdosta State University

Byron K. Brown
Valdosta State University

Houghton Mifflin Company ■ Boston   New York

Senior Sponsoring Editor: Dean Johnson
Senior Project Editor: Rosemary Winfield
Production Design Coordinator: Lisa Jelly
Senior Manufacturing Coordinator: Sally Culler
Senior Marketing Manager: Nancy Lyman

Contents

Sentence Structure   127

Punctuation   179

12. Commas   180

13. Unnecessary Commas   205

14. Semicolons, Colons, Dashes, Parentheses, and Brackets   213

15. Quotation Marks and End Punctuation   225

Mechanics   231

16. Underlining for Italics   232

Preface

The organization of the Seventh Edition of *Practical English Workbook* closely follows that of *Practical English Handbook,* Eleventh Edition. For those students who require more practice with basic skills, this workbook is designed to reinforce the instruction of the handbook with parallel lessons, additional examples, and varied exercises. Beginning with parts of speech, the workbook also provides lessons on parts of sentences, sentence errors, punctuation, mechanics, diction and style, and paragraphs. The logical sequence of these lessons makes *Practical English Workbook* adaptable to other texts as well as to independent study and laboratory instruction for students at all levels.

For the Seventh Edition we have undertaken a thorough revision of *Practical English Workbook.* We have

- improved all instructional sections, giving more contemporary examples and clearer, more complete coverage of grammatical points.
- revised most exercises for clarity and content.
- incorporated new material more closely related to the interests and concerns of a culturally diverse audience.

As with the Sixth Edition, we have kept the style concise and readable, avoiding the extremes of colloquialism and rigid formality. This edition, as did its predecessors, stresses clarity and precision.

Like *Practical English Handbook,* this edition of *Practical English Workbook* follows a traditional approach to grammar, punctuation, and syntax but also stresses the process of composition in the section on paragraphs. We believe that this method has proven itself over the years as the best means to call attention to writing problems and to improve students' writing skills. This mainstream approach to grammar, punctuation, and syntax has dictated the workbook's methodology. We have worked toward stating the most useful rules in the simplest form possible and again have stressed typical problems in both examples and exercises. Throughout the text, emphasis is upon building writing skills and developing the student's understanding of the well-established practices governing the use of the English language.

We wish to thank the following instructors for their critiques of the book: Anna Battigelli, SUNY–Plattsburgh; Jay Long, Baptist Bible College, PA.

F. C. W.

W. B. D.

J. T. H.

M. G. H.

B. B.

Grammar

1 The Parts of Speech

There are eight parts of speech in the English language: nouns, pronouns, verbs, adjectives, adverbs, conjunctions, prepositions, and interjections.

NOUNS

Nouns are words that name. There are five kinds of nouns: proper nouns, common nouns, collective nouns, abstract nouns, and concrete nouns.

- **Proper nouns** name particular persons, places, or things *(Thomas Edison, Chicago, Kleenex)*.

  Benjamin Franklin published *Poor Richard's Almanac* in *Philadelphia*.

- Common nouns name one or more of a class or group *(doctor, pilots, artists)*.

  Roger placed a *vase* of freshly cut *flowers* on the *table*.

- **Collective nouns** name a whole group, though they are singular in form *(senate, jury, clergy)*.

  The *jury* believes that the accused is innocent.

- **Abstract nouns** name concepts, beliefs, or qualities *(truth, energy, humor)*.

  Freedom implies *responsibility.*

- **Concrete nouns** name things experienced through the senses *(fire, coffee, roses)*.

  Hundreds of *acorns* littered the *ground* under the large *oak.*

PRONOUNS

There are seven kinds of pronouns. Most pronouns are used in place of nouns, although indefinite pronouns do not refer to any particular nouns.

- **Demonstrative pronouns** summarize in one word the content of a statement that has already been made. They can be singular *(this, that)* or plural *(these, those)*.

  Fruit, bran, whole wheat—*these* are common sources of healthful fiber.

- **Indefinite pronouns** do not indicate a particular person or thing. They are usually singular. The most common indefinite pronouns are *any, anybody, anyone, everybody, everyone, neither, none, one,* and *some.*

  Neither of her roommates shares her love of progressive jazz.

- **Intensive pronouns** end in *-self* or *-selves (herself, themselves)*. An intensive pronoun emphasizes a word that precedes it in the sentence.

  She *herself* was surprised at her quick success.

  The committee *itself* was confused.

- **Interrogative pronouns** *(what, which, who, whom, whose, whoever, whomever)* are used in questions.

  Who posted that notice on the bulletin board?

  What was the final score?

- **Personal pronouns** usually refer to a person or a group of people but may refer to an object or objects. They have many forms, depending on their grammatical function.

  Ask *her* whether *she* has called *him* yet.

  After *he* waxed *his* car, *he* parked *it* in the garage.

	SINGULAR	PLURAL
First person	I, me, mine	we, us, ours
Second person	you, yours	you, yours
Third person	he, she, it, him, her, his, hers, its	they, them, theirs

- **Reflexive pronouns** end in *-self* or *-selves* and indicate that the subject acts upon itself.

  He caught *himself* making the same mistake twice.

  The broken flywheel caused the machine to destroy *itself*.

- **Relative pronouns** *(who, whom, whoever, whomever, whichever, whose, that, what, which)* are used to introduce dependent adjective and noun clauses.

  You can eat the pie *that is in the refrigerator*. [adjective clause modifying *pie,* introduced by the relative pronoun *that*]

  Whoever visited the client needs to write the report. [noun clause used as subject of sentence]

VERBS

Verbs assert an action or express a condition.

  The bus *screeched* to a stop. [verb showing *action*]

  The capital of Missouri *is* Jefferson City. [verb showing *condition*]

3

Verbs that show *condition* are called **linking verbs.** The most common linking verbs are forms of the verb *to be (is, are, was, were)*. Other linking verbs are *seem, become, look, appear, feel, sound, smell,* and *taste*.

The music *is* discordant yet interesting.

Main verbs may have **auxiliary verbs,** or helpers, such as *are, have, may,* and *will*.

Renovation of the old house *may* take up to a year.

ADJECTIVES

Adjectives are descriptive words that modify nouns or pronouns. The **definite article** *the* and the **indefinite articles** *a* and *an* are also classified as adjectives.

The brilliant sunset left us breathless.

Predicate adjectives follow linking verbs and modify the subject of the sentence.

The article is *informative*.
The car looks *new*.

Some **possessive adjectives** have forms that are similar to possessive pronouns: *my, your, her, his, its, their*. These adjectives refer to specific nouns just as pronouns do, but they function as adjectives. *Your, our,* and *their* end with s in the pronoun form.

Your dinner is ready.
These gloves are *yours*.

Demonstrative adjectives and demonstrative pronouns have the same forms: *this, that, these, those*. (See demonstrative pronouns, p. 2.)

This comment is helpful. [*This* modifies *comment*.]
This is a helpful comment. [*This* is used here as a demonstrative pronoun.]

Indefinite adjectives resemble indefinite pronouns: *some, many, most, every*.

Every employee received a bonus. [*Every* modifies *employee*.]
Everyone left. [*Everyone* is an indefinite pronoun.]

ADVERBS

Adverbs describe, qualify, or limit verbs (and verbals), adjectives, and other adverbs.

The cashier laughed *uproariously.* [adverb—modifies a verb]

Be sure to read the instructions *carefully.* [adverb—modifies the verbal *to read*]

The train was *very* late. [adverb—modifies the adjective *late*]

We shall be through *very* soon. [adverb—modifies another adverb, *soon*]

Many adverbs are formed by adding *-ly* to adjectives; others express place or time: *soon, later, always, forever, there,* and *out.*

Bring the newspaper *inside.* [*Inside* expresses place.]

Bring me the newspaper *now.* [*Now* expresses time.]

CONJUNCTIVE ADVERBS

Conjunctive adverbs (*therefore, however, furthermore, moreover, consequently, thus,* etc.) connect clauses and phrases.

Fred tried to buy four tickets; *however,* the concert was already sold out. [*However* connects two independent clauses.]

CONJUNCTIONS

Conjunctions connect words, phrases, and clauses.

Coordinating conjunctions (*and, but, or, nor, for, yet, so*) connect sentence elements that are of equal rank.

Music boxes *and* bric-a-brac lined the shelves of the gift shop. [conjunction joining two nouns]

We called the apartment manager, *but* she was not at home. [conjunction joining two independent clauses]

Subordinating conjunctions introduce a dependent clause in a sentence—that is, one that cannot stand alone as a sentence. Some common subordinating conjunctions are *although, because, if, since, unless,* and *when.*

When we finished the test. [dependent element, not a sentence]

When we finished the test, we turned in our papers. [dependent element joined to independent clause to form a complete sentence]

We were tired *because we had studied all night.* [dependent element joined to independent clause to form a complete sentence]

PREPOSITIONS

Prepositions are connective words that join nouns or pronouns to other words in a sentence to form a unit (called a **prepositional phrase**). Prepositional phrases function as either adjectives or adverbs. Some prepositions are *above, at, before, by, from, in, into, of, over, through, up,* and *with.* Some groups of words (*according to, in spite of, along with*) may also function as prepositions.

The jet flew *through the clouds*. [*Through the clouds* is a prepositional phrase used as an adverb to modify the verb *flew.*]

The woman *in the car* is my mother. [*In the car* is a prepositional phrase used as an adjective to modify the noun *woman.*]

Some words that resemble prepositions function as adverbs:

Go out. [*out* used as adverb]

Go out the door. [*out* used as preposition]

Some words such as *before* and *after* may function as either prepositions or subordinating conjunctions.

INTERJECTIONS

Interjections are words that express surprise or strong emotions. They may stand alone or be part of a sentence. Interjections usually are avoided in formal writing.

Wow!

Well, you should have been more careful.

1.1 Nouns

Nouns are words that name. There are five kinds of nouns: proper nouns, common nouns, collective nouns, abstract nouns, and concrete nouns.

■ *Underline the nouns in the following sentences.*

EXAMPLES

Educational <u>television</u> needs private <u>donations</u>.

Marshall's coin <u>collection</u> is quite valuable.

<u>Bill Clinton</u> succeeded <u>George Bush</u> as <u>president</u> of the <u>United States</u>.

1. The picture of A. B. Peterson, who wrote the words to "Waltzing Matilda," appears on Australia's ten-dollar bill.

2. Many companies now offer maternity leaves for women, and some offer paternity leaves for men.

3. Email has dramatically expanded our ability to communicate with people all over the world.

4. Khadijah was Muhammad's first wife and, according to the Koran, one of the four perfect women.

5. Early in the twentieth century two hundred button factories in the United States almost depleted the supply of freshwater mussels.

6. At least two birds build their nests underground: the greater melampitta of New Guinea and the burrowing owl of North America.

7. The Galapagos Islands, volcanic in origin and isolated in the Pacific Ocean, offer many biological wonders.

8. In small doses, selenium is a necessary part of the human diet.

9. In 1988, divers off the coast of Turkey found jars of baked clay dating from the thirteenth century B.C.

10. Generally speaking, babies born at sea level weigh more than babies born at higher altitudes.

1.2 Pronouns

There are seven kinds of pronouns: demonstrative, indefinite, intensive, interrogative, reflexive, relative, and personal. Most pronouns are used in place of nouns, although indefinite pronouns do not refer to any particular noun.

■ *Underline the pronouns in the following sentences.*

EXAMPLES

She herself intends to represent the clients. [personal, intensive pronouns]

Students who want to view the art exhibit will find it in Roswell Hall, which is next to the library. [relative, personal, relative pronouns]

Meg wants everyone to try her new recipe. [indefinite, personal (possessive) pronouns]

1. Nobody spoke against the proposal, but each of us had reasons to object to it.

2. Fax machines allow us to send copies of documents almost as quickly as we can place a telephone call.

3. In an aquafarm, lobsters can reach one pound in a month; in the sea, they need six months to reach that weight.

4. Wetlands provide the ecological bases for wildlife; however, they are quite vulnerable to development, which has destroyed most of them in the continental United States.

5. Most of the nation's small businesses are quite concerned about rising costs for their employees' health insurance.

6. Signaling to those who steadied her ladder, the firefighter began her long descent.

7. Some chicks take up to two days to free themselves from their shells.

8. Fighting fatigue and frostbite, the climbers built themselves a snow cave and tried to dry some of their clothing.

9. Street vendors peddle their wares to anyone who will buy them.

10. Few know that Mark Twain was the first person to write a novel on a typewriter. It was *Tom Sawyer*.

1.3 Verbs

Verbs assert an action or express a condition. Verbs that show *condition* are called **linking verbs.** The most common linking verbs are forms of the verb *to be (is, are, was, were).* Other linking verbs are *seem, become, look, appear, feel, sound, smell,* and *taste.*

Main verbs may have **auxiliary verbs,** or helpers, such as *are, have, may,* and *will.*

■ *Underline the verbs in the following sentences.*

EXAMPLES

Technology <u>raises</u> hope for greater crop yields. [action verb]

The world's largest computer exhibit <u>is held</u> annually in Hannover, Germany.

Economists <u>have become</u> less optimistic about the recovery. [auxiliary verb and linking verb showing condition]

1. Brazilians celebrate Christmas with fireworks.

2. While serving as president, Herbert Hoover gave all of his salary to charity.

3. Many collectors especially value Dresden china.

4. Cold water weighs less than hot water.

5. Several famous directors will attend the festival of documentary films in London.

6. People once assumed that a toothache was a sign that some god was angry.

7. Some scientists believe that the earth's ozone layer is being destroyed; others disagree.

8. The president of the United States appoints federal judges, who have life tenures.

9. The tail of a comet always points away from the sun.

10. On the American frontier, physicians set broken bones, delivered babies, pulled teeth, and inspected water supplies.

1.4 Adjectives

Adjectives are descriptive words that modify nouns or pronouns. The **definite article** *the* and the **indefinite articles** *a* and *an* are also classified as adjectives. There are four types of adjectives: predicate, possessive, demonstrative, and indefinite.

■ *Underline the adjectives in the following sentences. Remember that articles* (a, an, the) *are also classified as adjectives.*

EXAMPLES

Most economists believe that a truly global economy has arrived.

Many new word-processing programs are extremely versatile. [Predicate adjective follows the linking verb *are*.]

1. The human body has about sixty thousand miles of blood vessels.

2. In ancient Greece, both men and women occasionally dyed their hair blonde.

3. In 1993, a small hurricane struck the barrier islands off the Carolinas during the tourist season.

4. Distance runners over thirty-five often are faster than they were fifteen years before.

5. Some collectors of baseball memorabilia would pay as much as $30,000 for a 1971 Mets jersey.

6. Every year, hundreds of bicyclists compete in the Tour de France, hoping to win the yellow jersey.

7. Some specialists in foreign languages find permanent employment in the field of diplomacy or in the arena of international business.

8. The semiprecious stones called garnets may be red, green, yellow, or white, among other colors.

9. Coral reefs are as dangerous as they are interesting.

10. A professional photographer's shots of world-famous celebrities often become collector's items.

1.5 Adverbs

Adverbs describe, qualify, or limit verbs (and verbals), adjectives, and other adverbs. Many adverbs are formed by adding *-ly* to adjectives; others express place or time.

■ *Underline the adverbs in the following sentences.*

EXAMPLES

Barge traffic on major waterways <u>usually</u> decreases during periods of <u>extremely</u> low water. [adverb modifying a verb and adverb modifying an adjective]

The news is <u>almost completely</u> certain to arouse controversy. [adverb modifying another adverb and adverb modifying an adjective]

1. Online bookstores offer a wide selection of titles, including popular CDs and tapes as well as books.

2. Many "concept cars" are enthusiastically praised at special car shows; however, few of them ever reach production.

3. Today's developer often tries to save as many trees as possible; lots that are shaded sell relatively quickly.

4. Physicists have often speculated, and almost always disagreed, about the size of the universe.

5. Service at fine restaurants sometimes takes a little longer when entrees must be individually prepared.

6. The smallest diamonds are often the clearest and sometimes the most finely cut.

7. While carefully examining the walls of the ancient building, the archaeologist suddenly discovered a small cache of coins that were easily two thousand years old.

8. The flowers were partially covered by a late spring frost that quickly melted when the sun rose.

9. In the middle of an exquisitely graceful performance, the figure skater suddenly stumbled and then fell heavily to the ice.

10. As the airplane descended gradually through the clouds, the pilot glanced quickly at the rapidly falling fuel gauge.

1.6 Conjunctions, Prepositions, and Interjections

Conjunctions connect words, phrases, and clauses. There are two types of conjunctions: **coordinating** and **subordinating conjunctions.**

Prepositions are connective words that join nouns or pronouns to other words in a sentence to form a unit (called a **prepositional phrase**). Prepositions function as either adjectives or adverbs.

Interjections are words that express surprise or strong emotions. They may stand alone or be part of a sentence.

■ *In the following sentences underline prepositions once, conjunctions twice, and interjections three times.*

EXAMPLES

"Oh," said the novelist, "I found that the first and last chapters of the novel were the most difficult to write." [interjection, coordinating conjunction, preposition]

Although the winds were strong, the boaters began the race for the gold cup. [subordinating conjunction, preposition]

1. The United States Senate has sixteen standing committees, and the House of Representatives has twenty-two.

2. When inventors receive a patent from the United States government, they may exclude all others from making, using, or selling the product of their imagination.

3. Although its exact whereabouts are unknown, somewhere in the Dragoon Mountains lies the burial spot of Cochise, chief of the Chiricahua Apaches.

4. Flamingos are pink because they eat so many shrimp.

5. Many people think that smallpox is not a modern disease, but it killed 300 million people during the twentieth century.

6. "Eureka! I found it!" are the most famous words ever uttered by Archimedes, a well-known scientist of ancient Greece.

7. Although Alfred Hitchcock's *Psycho* cost only $800,000 to film, it earned more than $40,000,000.

8. "No!" responded the officer. "I will not follow that order!"

9. The fans went home early because none of them wanted to see their team lose so badly.

10. People do not seem to realize the need to conserve natural resources, nor do they comprehend the consequences if they do not.

1.7 Same Word; Several Functions

■ *Many words can function as several parts of speech. Compose very brief sentences with the following words, illustrating the parts of speech in parentheses. If necessary, check a dictionary.*

EXAMPLES
right (noun) *Could the defendant tell the difference between right and wrong?*

(adjective) *The right side of the highway was beautiful in its spring colors.*

(adverb) *The new attorney rose right to the top of his profession.*

1. mean (verb) _____

_____

_____

(adjective) _____

_____

_____

(noun) _____

_____

_____

2. water (noun) _____

_____

_____

(verb) _____

_____

_____

(adjective) _____

_____

_____

3. well (noun) _____

_____

_____

(interjection) _____

_____

_____

(adverb) _____

_____

_____

4. spring (noun) _____

_____

_____

(verb) _____

_____

_____

(adjective) _____

_____

_____

5. light (noun) _____

_____

_____

(adjective) _____

_____

(verb) _____

_____

_____

6. treasure (noun) _____

_____

_____

(verb) _____

_____

(adjective) _____

_____

_____

7. total (noun) _____

_____

_____

(adjective) _____

_____

_____

(verb) _____

_____

_____

8. second (adjective) _____

_____

_____

(verb) _____

_____

_____

(adverb) _____

_____

_____

9. fast (adjective) _____

_____

_____

(adverb) _____

_____

_____

(verb) _____

_____

_____

10. down (noun) _____

_____

_____

(verb) _____

_____

_____

(preposition) _____

_____

_____

1.8 Parts of Speech: Review 1

■ *Identify the part of speech of each italicized word.*

When lawyers are criticized for defending criminals, *their* critics often *overlook* a crucial fact: people charged *with* crimes are not *always* guilty of those crimes. The U.S. legal system, which is based on *the* principle that those accused of breaking the *law* shall be regarded as innocent until proven guilty, *was* designed to protect *innocent* people from unjust treatment. By serving as advocates for the accused, *attorneys play* an important role in guaranteeing the rights of *those* brought to trial. One result, *unfortunately,* is that those *who* are guilty of crimes must also be treated as if they are innocent until *they* have been convicted in *a* court of law. Put simply, *one* justification for such a procedure is that it is better to let *some criminals* escape *justice* than to unjustly punish an innocent person.

1.9 Parts of Speech: Review 2

■ *Identify the part of speech of each italicized word.*

Venice, *one* of Europe's most *famous* cities, is *slowly* becoming flooded.

The sea level *near* the city *has* risen *over* four inches in the past century.

Worse yet, the land upon *which* it is built has sunk at least eight *inches.* Ex-

perts *predict* that *global* sea levels will rise *another* eight inches by the year

2050. *If* that *happens,* the city's *famed* waterways will *inundate* the city for

six *months* each year. Needless to say, *these* predictions have alarmed the

city's leaders, *and* several *plans* to save *Venice* have been proposed.

2 The Parts of Sentences

Sentences are built of several distinct grammatical elements. All sentences must have a subject and a predicate, combined in what is called an independent clause. This basic unit can be expanded by adding complements, phrases, verbals, and other clauses.

SUBJECTS AND PREDICATES

A sentence has a complete meaning and can stand on its own. Its essential parts are its subject and predicate.

The **subject** does something, has something done to it, or is described.

> The *woman* is reading. [subject acting]
>
> *Books* are read. [subject acted upon]
>
> *Books* are interesting. [subject described]

In sentences that command, a subject may be understood, even though it does not literally appear in the sentence.

> Bring me some coffee. [*You* is the understood subject.]

A **simple subject** usually consists of one word.

> The *house* is dark. [simple subject]

The **complete subject** consists of all the words that function together as the subject.

> *The old house* is dark. [complete subject]

The **predicate** says something about the subject.

> The woman *is reading.*
>
> Encyclopedias *are handy sources of information.*
>
> Everyone *knew the answer to the problem.*

The verb in a sentence is called the **simple predicate.**

> They *watched* the movie.

The simple predicate, its modifiers, and any complements are together called the **complete predicate.**

> Jack *finished eating his dinner.*

Similar units of a sentence may be linked together and function together as **compound subjects** or **compound predicates.**

> *Phil* and *Steve* enjoy scuba diving. [compound subject]

Amy *bought* her ticket and *took* a seat. [compound predicate]

The *Italians* and the *Brazilians* both *love* soccer fanatically and *play* it brilliantly. [compound subject and compound predicate]

COMPLEMENTS

Complements are words added to complete the meaning of some sentences. They can be predicate adjectives, predicate nominatives, direct objects, or indirect objects.

Predicate adjectives are adjectives that follow linking verbs and describe the subject.

Her voice is *beautiful*. [*Beautiful* describes *voice*.]

Some problems seem *insoluble*. [*Insoluble* describes *problems*.]

Predicate nominatives are nouns that follow linking verbs and rename the subject.

Tonight's lecturer is a *psychologist*. [*Psychologist* renames *lecturer*.]

Predicate adjectives and predicate nominatives are also called **subjective complements.**

Direct objects receive the action of a transitive verb directly.

We played *Scrabble*. [direct object telling what *we* played]

The soldiers brought *water*. [direct object telling what *the soldiers* brought]

Indirect objects, which receive the action of the verb indirectly, appear in front of direct objects. The prepositions *to* or *for* are understood though they do not appear in the sentence.

The soldiers brought *us* water. [indirect object telling *to whom* the soldiers brought water]

He did *her* a great favor. [indirect object telling *for whom* he did the favor]

Objective complements accompany direct objects to complete the meaning of the sentence. They may modify the direct object or be synonymous with it.

The new owner painted his house *red*. [objective complement modifying the direct object]

Her grandchildren call her *Mimi*. [objective complement synonymous with the direct object]

PHRASES

A phrase is a group of words that lacks either a subject or a predicate. A phrase does not express a complete thought; therefore, it is not a sentence. A **noun phrase** consists of a noun and its modifiers.

A graceful old elm towered over the house.

30

An **appositive phrase** renames a noun.

> George, *our new office manager,* met with his staff this morning.

A **verb phrase** consists of the main verb and its helping verbs.

> The house *is being painted.*

Prepositional phrases begin with prepositions and function as adjectives or adverbs.

> The door *to the closet* is open. [functions as an adjective to modify *door*]
> The snow fell *in huge flakes.* [functions as an adverb to modify *fell*]

VERBALS AND VERBAL PHRASES

A **verbal** is formed from a verb. There are three kinds of verbals: gerunds, participles, and infinitives. A verbal and the words associated with it compose a **verbal phrase.**

Gerunds

A gerund ends in *-ing.* Gerunds and gerund phrases always function as nouns.

> *Hiking* is fun. [gerund as subject]
> *Hiking the Appalachian Trail* is fun. [gerund phrase as subject.]
> Before *hiking the Appalachian Trail,* we carefully studied the map. [gerund phrase as the object of a preposition]

Participles

Participles usually end in *-ing, -ed, -d, -t,* or *-n.* Participles and participial phrases function as adjectives.

> *Freezing* rain made the roads treacherous. [participle modifying *rain*]
> The mechanic replaced the *dented* fender. [participle modifying *fender*]
> *Realizing that they were lost,* the hikers began to panic. [participial phrase modifying *hikers*]

Infinitives

Infinitives usually begin with *to,* which is followed by a verb. They function as nouns, adjectives, or adverbs.

> *To show the new student around our school* took time. [infinitive phrase as noun (subject)]
> Camera cases *to be carried on the trip* must be waterproof. [infinitive phrase as adjective]
> *To be certain of lodging,* one should make reservations. [infinitive phrase as adverb]
> The children helped their father *plant the garden.* [infinitive phrase without *to* as adverb]

CLAUSES

Clauses are groups of words with both subjects and predicates. Clauses are either independent or dependent (sometimes called *subordinate*). **Independent clauses** may stand alone as complete sentences. Two or more of them may be linked by (1) a comma with a **coordinating conjunction** *(and, but, or, nor, for, so, yet)*, (2) a semicolon, (3) a semicolon with a **conjunctive adverb** (such as *however, therefore, moreover, nevertheless, otherwise*) followed by a comma, or (4) a colon.

> The circus is over, *and* the workers are cleaning the grounds. [two independent clauses connected by a comma and a coordinating conjunction]

> The auditorium was packed; people were standing in the aisles. [two independent clauses connected by a semicolon]

> Low clouds obscured much of the mountain; *however,* the snow-capped peak sparkled in the bright sunlight. [two independent clauses joined by a semicolon with a conjunctive adverb and a comma]

> The judge refused to hear the case: his brother was the defendant. [two independent clauses connected by a colon]

Dependent clauses (also called **subordinate clauses**) cannot stand alone since they do not express complete thoughts. However, these clauses can function as nouns, adjectives, or adverbs.

> *Who the next chairman will be* remains a secret. [noun clause as subject]

> The salesman *who opened the most new accounts* won a trip to the Bahamas. [adjective clause modifying *salesman*]

> *When the master of ceremonies announced the winner,* the audience applauded enthusiastically. [adverb clause modifying *applauded*]

EXPANDING AND COMBINING CLAUSES

A series of short independent clauses can be combined into longer, more sophisticated sentences by transforming most of them into different kinds of phrases and clauses.

> Cocker spaniels are very popular in America.
>
> They are popular as pets.
>
> They are popular as show dogs.
>
> They are named for their ability to hunt woodcocks.
>
> Woodcocks are a type of game bird.

> Named for their ability to hunt woodcocks [past participle phrase], a type of game bird [appositive phrase], cocker spaniels are very popular in America [independent clause] as pets and show dogs [prepositional phrase].

> or

> Cocker spaniels, which are very popular in America as pets and show dogs, are named for their ability to hunt a type of game bird called a woodcock.

2.1 The Parts of Sentences

■ *Underline the simple or compound subjects once and the simple or compound predicates twice. Identify complements by placing the abbreviations **p.a.** (predicate adjective—follows linking verbs and describes the subject), **p.n.** (predicate nominative—follows linking verbs and renames the subject), **d.o.** (direct object—receives the action of a transitive verb), **i.o.** (indirect object—indirectly receives the action of the verb), and **o.c.** (objective complement—modifies or is synonymous with the direct object) above the appropriate words.*

EXAMPLES

d.o.
Silicon chips have revolutionized the electronics industry.

i.o.   *d.o.*
Geologists gave investors the preliminary analysis of several oil wells.

d.o. o.c.
Allison and Chris painted their room blue.

1. Drip irrigation is a very efficient method of watering a garden.

2. Cemeteries in New Orleans contain many above-ground tombs.

3. Physicians sometimes prescribe low-sodium diets for older patients.

4. Similes and metaphors are commonly used figures of speech.

5. Franklin Delano Roosevelt won four presidential elections.

6. In 1856, Gail Borden, a fifty-four-year-old inventor, discovered a way to keep milk from spoiling and soon became rich.

7. Spanish treasure ships laden with gold, silver, and gems are still being discovered in the Caribbean.

8. At air shows stunt pilots put their planes into steep power stalls and then slip into dives.

9. Although birds have been marked in various ways since the Roman Empire, scientific bird banding did not become common until the beginning of the twentieth century.

10. Scorpions, rattlesnakes, gila monsters, and black widow spiders inhabit the deserts of Arizona.

2.2 The Parts of Sentences

■ *Underline the simple or compound subjects once and the simple or compound predi-*
cates twice. Identify complements by placing the abbreviations **p.a.** *(predicate adjec-*
tive—follows linking verbs and describes the subject), **p.n.** *(predicate nominative—fol-*
lows linking verbs and renames the subject), **d.o.** *(direct object—receives the action of*
a transitive verb), **i.o.** *(indirect object—indirectly receives the action of the verb), and*
o.c. *(objective complement—modifies or is synonymous with the direct object) above*
the appropriate words.

EXAMPLES
                                              p.a.
Those slides of the ancient Incan ruins were fascinating.

         p.n.
She became president of the holding company last week.

1. The statues of ancient Egypt continue to surprise and amaze us.

2. Some of them are carved out of anorthosite gneiss, which glows
   deep blue in the sunlight.

3. Some are huge, commemorating the power and accomplishments of
   pharaohs.

4. Many royal tombs contain dozens of small statues intended to serve
   the deceased in the afterlife.

5. Life-sized statues, astonishingly realistic and beautifully painted,
   served as repositories of the *ka,* or soul, of the dead.

6. Priests brought these statues ritual foods and other offerings.

7. A few tombs contain finely sculptured heads, which may have
   served as spares or which may have been used in magical rites.

Adapted from Bennett Schiff, "Out of Egypt: Art in the Age of the Pyramids,"
Smithsonian 30, no. 6 (1999): 108–119.

2.3 Phrases

A **noun phrase** consists of a noun and its modifiers. An **appositive phrase** renames a noun. A **verb phrase** consists of the main verb and its helping verbs. **Prepositional phrases** begin with prepositions and function as adjectives or adverbs.

■ *Identify each of the following italicized phrases as a noun phrase, an appositive phrase, a verb phrase, or a prepositional phrase.*

EXAMPLES

The Alamo, *an old Spanish mission in San Antonio,* was the site of a famous battle during the Texas War of Independence.

appositive phrase

Some of the students *have been considering* camping out all night at the door of the ticket office.

verb phrase

Influenza epidemics killed many Americans *at the end of the First World War.*

two prepositional phrases

1. The native religion of Japan is called Shinto, *a word that means "the way of gods."*

   _____

2. *Between 1986 and 1992,* the percentage of all record sales represented by rock music fell from 47 percent to 36 percent.

   _____

3. Celebration, Florida, *a town planned and built by the Disney corporation,* has inspired at least two books.

   _____

4. *Many war-game enthusiasts* re-create battles of the past by using miniature soldiers and carefully reconstructed battlefields.

   _____

5. He took *his lawn mower* to a small but very popular repair shop recommended by his neighbor.

   _____

6. Steven Spielberg has directed *several of the most profitable films ever made.*

   _____

7. The first subway was built in London *between 1860 and 1863.*

   _____

8. Stephen King became one *of the most popular modern American writers.*

_____

9. Surprisingly, more nonnative plants grow *in New York* than grow in California.

_____

10. A mother and two children survived the tornado *by taking shelter in their bathtub.*

_____

2.4 Phrases

A **noun phrase** consists of a noun and its modifiers. A **modifier** can be either an appositive phrase (which renames a noun) or a prepositional phrase (which functions as an adjective or adverb). A **verbal phrase** is formed from a verb. There are three kinds of verbals: gerunds, participles, and infinitives. A **verb phrase** consists of the main verb and its helping verbs.

■ *Indicate whether the italicized phrase is used as a noun, modifier, verbal, or verb and indicate its function in the sentence.*

EXAMPLES

Using credit cards is a way *of life* for modern Americans.

modifier — prepositional phrase used as adjective modifying noun way

The scientists, concerned about the potential hazards, wanted the latest research findings made public.

verbal — participial phrase used as adjective modifying noun scientists

Keeping their bodies in good condition is a primary concern of many young Americans.

verbal — gerund phrase used as noun (subject of is)

1. Alchemists *of the Middle Ages* tried to transform lead into gold.

   _____

2. *Best known for such children's classics as The Cat in the Hat and Green Eggs and Ham,* Theodore Seuss Geisel, or Dr. Seuss, won a Pulitzer Prize for a series of anti-Fascist cartoons published between 1941 and 1942.

   _____

3. Toni Morrison, *winner of the 1993 Nobel Prize for literature,* grew up in Arkansas.

_____

4. They wanted *to eat* at the Indonesian restaurant.

_____

5. *Blushing deeply* and favoring a twisted ankle, the dancer left the stage.

_____

6. The chinook winds whip down the eastern slopes of the Rocky Mountains and sweep *across the vast prairies.*

_____

7. *The first air-conditioned car* was the 1939 Packard.

_____

8. The average third-grader in the United States spends about 900 hours a year in class and 1,170 hours a year *watching television.*

_____

9. The ocean floor *still has not been fully explored.*

_____

10. *The tour bus* stopped in Savannah so that the tourists could visit the beautiful old homes that date back to the last part of the eighteenth century.

_____

2.5 Verbal Phrases

A verbal phrase is formed from a verb. There are three kinds of verbals. A **gerund** always ends in *-ing* and functions as a noun. **Participles** usually end in *-ing, -ed, -d, -t,* or *-n* and function as adjectives. **Infinitives** usually begin with *to,* which is followed by a verb, and function as nouns, adjectives, or adverbs.

■ *Underline verbal phrases in the following sentences. Identify the verbal phrase as participial, infinitive, or gerund; its part of speech; and its function.*

EXAMPLES
Stretching for several blocks, the traffic jam tested the drivers' patience.

participial phrase used as adjective to modify traffic jam

To visit the Baseball Hall of Fame is every young boy's dream.

infinitive phrase (noun) used as subject of verb is

We plan *to finish the project by September*.

infinitive phrase (noun) used as direct object of verb plan

1. Dying at a rate of about one species each 1,000 years, dinosaurs during the "great dying" actually took 50 to 75 million years to become extinct.

_____

2. To awaken every morning at 4:00 A.M., Levi Hutchins invented the alarm clock in 1787.

_____

3. Ardent fans try to move closer to the front of the auditorium.

_____

4. Constructed in 1885, the old house had a special charm about it.

_____

5. Scientists have been able to find links between left-handedness and a number of diseases.

_____

6. Trained to hunt small burrowing animals, the dachshund did not originate in Germany but rather in Egypt.

_____

7. Brazil, motivated by the need for an additional energy source, has produced gasohol from sugar as a viable alternative to gasoline.

_____

8. Now spanning a short canal off the Colorado River, London Bridge is no longer falling down.

_____

9. The tourists wanted to revisit the Arch of Triumph and the Eiffel Tower before they left Paris.

_____

10. Founded in 1933, Black Mountain College lasted only twenty-three years.

_____

11. To reach the top of the Eiffel Tower, one would have to climb 1,792 steps.

_____

12. The chef, trying to impress his more sophisticated customers, served strawberry soup as an appetizer.

_____

13. Finishing the last chapter of her novel was much more difficult than she had expected.

_____

14. Gertrude Ederle was the first woman to swim the English Channel.

_____

15. Wanting to honor Louis Sockalexis, the first Native American to play professional baseball, the Cleveland Naps changed their name to the Cleveland Indians in 1914.

_____

16. Borrowing an idea from European law enforcement, some U.S. state police units are now using cameras to catch speeders.

_____

17. Learning how emotions influence behavior is a major goal of psychology.

_____

18. Archaeologists working under strenuous conditions in the Arctic discovered toy dolls over five hundred years old.

_____

19. To enjoy television, a couch potato needs a comfortable couch, a variety of snacks, and a remote control.

_____

20. Some sand dunes found in southwestern France stand 350 feet high.

_____

2.6 Clauses

An **independent clause** stands alone as a complete sentence. A **dependent** or **subordinate clause** cannot stand as a complete sentence and functions as a noun, an adjective, or an adverb.

■ *Write whether the italicized dependent clauses are used as nouns, adjectives, or adverbs. Remember that dependent clauses can be parts of independent clauses.*

EXAMPLES

Although computers are now a fact of life, many people are afraid to use them.   *adverb*

What the speaker said could be heard. [dependent clause used as subject of independent clause]   *noun*

The compact car *that establishes a reputation for quality* will always have a good market.   *adjective*

1. Jacques Cousteau invented the aqualung *while he was a member of the French Underground during World War II.*   _____

2. *While Samuel Johnson compiled his famous dictionary,* he employed the services of four assistants.   _____

3. Ice cream, *which was commercially made as early as 1786,* was first sold in New York.   _____

4. *Although the porpoise is a graceful animal,* its name is derived from two Latin words meaning "pig fish."   _____

5. *Although the King Ranch in Texas contains over one million acres,* it was the first ranch to be completely fenced in.   _____

6. The ancient Romans thought *that a crooked nose was a sign of leadership ability.*   _____

7. The foul weather *that had been expected for a week* finally arrived.   _____

8. *Before they receive a black belt in tae kwon do,* students must master nine forms, successfully spar with two opponents, and break two boards. _____

9. *Since we moved to town*, five new families have moved into our neighborhood. _____

10. *When the young reporter arrived*, she interviewed several celebrities. _____

11. *How Houdini performed many of his amazing feats* remains a mystery. _____

12. John Milton was already totally blind *when he began composing his epic poem* Paradise Lost. _____

13. She advertised for a housekeeper *who would shop for groceries, prepare meals, and do laundry.* _____

14. *While John scouted downstream for dangerous rapids*, Beth tried to repair the raft. _____

15. Megan accepted an offer to play professional basketball in France *although she would have preferred to stay in the United States.* _____

16. *After the Berlin Wall fell in 1989*, a reunited Germany faced several serious economic problems. _____

17. The Internet has profoundly changed the ways *that stocks are bought and sold.* _____

18. Hawaii is the only one of the United States *that produces coffee.* _____

19. Anyone *who decides to run for president of the United States* must file a financial statement with the Federal Election Commission. _____

20. *How he could afford to repair the dilapidated mansion* was a complete mystery to his friends. _____

2.7 Phrases and Clauses: Review 1

■ *Identify the type of each italicized phrase and clause.*

There are many theories about the fate of dinosaurs, (1) *the largest animals ever to walk the earth.* After (2) *existing for thousands of years,* (3) *these magnificent reptiles* suddenly disappeared (4) *without a trace.* Some archaeologists (5) *who have also studied astronomy* believe that a giant meteor hit the earth, stirring clouds of dust that blocked the sunlight, causing plants and then dinosaurs to die. (6) *Other scientists see another possible cause.* They believe that a major volcanic eruption, (7) *with a single massive blast,* could have produced enough ash to block the sun for years. (8) *Basing their opinions on data derived from space exploration and from recent volcanic activity on the earth,* many scientists believe that the dinosaurs disappeared so quickly that their fate had to be the result of a single catastrophe. (9) *To learn more,* these scientists (10) *are continuing* their collaborative efforts.

1. _____

2. _____

3. _____

4. _____

5. _____

6. _____

7. _____

8. _____

9. _____

10. _____

2.8 Phrases and Clauses: Review 2

■ *Use phrases, coordinating conjunctions, subordinating conjunctions, and conjunctive adverbs to connect the following clauses. Each cluster of clauses should be combined into a single sentence.*

EXAMPLE:

1. The *Mona Lisa* is famous.
2. She is famous for her unusual smile.
3. The reason for her unusual smile will never be known.
4. Experts have suggested many possible reasons.
5. They believe she might have had poor teeth.
6. They believe she might have had cerebral palsy.
7. They believe she might have had a stroke.

Although the reason for the *Mona Lisa*'s unusual smile will never be known, experts believe that poor teeth, cerebral palsy, or even a stroke may explain the enigmatic expression that made her famous.

1. Temujin was born.
2. He was born at some time in the 1160s.
3. He was born in northeastern Mongolia.
4. He was the son of a chief.
5. The chief was poisoned by a rival tribe.

6. Temujin was a young man.
7. When he was young, Temujin united several tribes.
8. He destroyed the Taters.
9. The Taters were a tribe.
10. The tribe poisoned his father.

11. In 1206, the Mongol tribes met.
12. At this meeting they named Temujin Genghis Khan.
13. Genghis Khan means "strong ruler."

14. Soon after, Genghis Khan invaded China.
15. He left with immense treasure.
16. He left with a new wife.
17. He left with 30,000 skilled workers.

18. He conquered other cities.
19. These cities were in central Asia.
20. These cities included Bukhara.
21. They included Samarkand.
22. They included Heart.
23. The Khan's troops circled the Caspian Sea.
24. They captured many Russian cities.

25. Genghis Khan died in 1227.
26. The people he conquered called him many things.
27. His people called him another thing.
28. They called him father of their country.

Adapted from Mike Edwards, "Lord of the Mongols: Genghis Khan," *National Geographic* 190, no. 6 (December 1996): 2–37.

3 The Kinds of Sentences

There are four kinds of sentences: simple, compound, complex, and compound-complex.

A **simple sentence** has one independent clause.

> The antismoking lobby is becoming increasingly powerful. [one subject, one predicate]
>
> Many airlines as well as other businesses have imposed and enforced strict antismoking regulations. [compound subject, compound predicate]

A **compound sentence** contains two or more independent clauses joined by a coordinating conjunction or a semicolon.

> The new art show at the museum opened today, and the crowd was immense. [two independent clauses joined by *and*]
>
> The new art show at the museum opened today; the crowd was immense. [two independent clauses joined by a semicolon]

A **complex sentence** consists of one independent clause and one or more dependent clauses.

> After the sudden thunderstorm ended, the streets were filled with water. [dependent clause and independent clause]

A **compound-complex sentence** is a compound sentence with one or more dependent clauses.

> After the sudden thunderstorm ended, the streets were filled with water, so traffic was stalled for nearly two hours. [dependent clause, then two independent clauses joined by the coordinating conjunction *so*]

3.1 Kinds of Sentences

■ *Identify each of the following sentences as simple* (**s**), *compound* (**cd**), *complex* (**cx**), *or compound-complex* (**cd/cx**).

EXAMPLES

_____*s*_____   Everyone visiting Los Angeles should visit Disneyland.

_____*cd*_____   We ordered a pepperoni pizza, but the restaurant delivered one topped with anchovies and black olives.

_____*cx*_____   Nurseries that wholesale Christmas trees increase their off-season income.

_____*cd/cx*_____   Small pickup trucks, which are now popular in urban areas, are practical for the small business, and they outsell many larger models.

_____   1. In 1847, Theobald Boehm designed the modern flute.

_____   2. Hybrid bicycles, which can be very expensive, are a cross between mountain bicycles and racers; some cyclists refer to them as cross-terrain models.

_____   3. Some adventurous climbers use ice axes, spiked boots, and crampons to scale frozen waterfalls, but their success depends on skill, stamina, and steady nerves.

_____   4. Moving south through Vermont, New Hampshire, Massachusetts, and Connecticut, the Connecticut River reaches the Atlantic Ocean.

_____   5. D. W. Griffith directed over four hundred one-reel films between 1908 and 1913.

_____   6. African termites, which dig as deep as 250 feet in search of water, sometimes bring particles of gold to the surface, and ancient African miners examined their mounds to find deposits of gold.

_____   7. The fourth largest pyramid in the world is not in Egypt but instead in Las Vegas.

_____ 8. Large amounts of fresh water pouring into the ocean from flooded rivers can hurt some forms of sea life, especially shellfish.

_____ 9. Many people believe that King Arthur, who supposedly ruled at Camelot, was a real person, but no conclusive proof for his existence has yet been confirmed.

_____ 10. Poland's Wieliczka salt mine, which has been in use since the 1200s, contains many beautiful sculptures carved from the salt by generations of miners.

NAME _____

DATE _____ SCORE _____

3.2 Kinds of Sentences

■ *Label the sentences in the following paragraph as simple **(s)**, compound **(cd)**, complex **(cx)**, or compound/complex **(cd/cx)**.*

1. Korea has many interesting sites. 2. The Kumgansan Mountains of North Korea rival the Alps in beauty, whereas the Hallyosula Waterway, located off the southern coast, contains many picturesque islands. 3. It is also the place where Admiral Yi, one of Korea's greatest war heroes, developed the first ironclad warships used in battle. 4. The Emille Bell, which was cast in A. D. 771, stands over eleven feet high, and it contains twenty-five tons of copper. 5. Every year, thousands of tourists from all over the world visit the Kyougiu National Museum as well as other sites to enjoy this ancient nation's cultural heritage.

3.3 Kinds of Sentences

■ *Write a brief paragraph on a topic of your choice. Use at least one simple sentence, one compound sentence, one complex sentence, and one compound-complex sentence. Label each kind of sentence in the margin.*

_____

_____

_____

_____

_____

_____

_____

_____

Sentence Errors

4 Common Sentence Errors

SENTENCE FRAGMENTS

Sentence fragments are incomplete sentences. They usually consist of phrases, dependent clauses, or any other word groups that are punctuated like sentences but that do not form complete thoughts.

INCORRECT

> Jason looked for seats near the fifty-yard line. So that he could see the football game better. [complete sentence followed by a sentence fragment (dependent clause punctuated as if it were a complete sentence)]

To correct fragments, rewrite them as independent clauses or attach them to complete sentences.

CORRECTED

> Jason looked for seats near the fifty-yard line. He could see the football game better from here. [sentence fragment turned into a complete sentence (independent clause) by removing subordinating conjunction *so that*]

> Jason looked for seats near the fifty-yard line so that he could see the football game better. [sentence fragment attached to a complete sentence as a dependent clause]

COMMAS SPLICES AND FUSED SENTENCES

A **fused** (or **run-on**) **sentence** occurs when two independent clauses have neither punctuation nor a conjunction connecting them.

INCORRECT

> No one saw the van the bank robbers drove it to Mexico.

> The movie was very exciting we discussed it on the way home.

> Tom never saw Alice again he often wondered what had happened to her.

A **comma splice** (also called a **comma fault**)) occurs when a comma alone is used to connect two independent clauses.

INCORRECT

> No one saw the van, the bank robbers drove it to Mexico.

> The movie was very exciting, we discussed it on the way home.

> Tom never saw Alice again, he often wondered what had happened to her.

Fused sentences and comma splices can be corrected in several ways:

1. Separate the independent clauses into separate sentences.

CORRECTED

No one saw the van. The bank robbers drove it to Mexico.

The movie was very exciting. We discussed it on the way home.

Tom never saw Alice again. He often wondered what had happened to her.

2. Use a semicolon to separate the independent clauses.

CORRECTED

No one saw the van; the bank robbers drove it to Mexico.

The movie was very exciting; we discussed it on the way home.

Tom never saw Alice again; he often wondered what had happened to her.

3. Separate the independent clauses with a comma and an appropriate coordinating conjunction.

CORRECTED

No one saw the van, *so* the bank robbers drove it to Mexico.

The movie was very exciting, *and* we discussed it on the way home.

Tom never saw Alice again, *yet* he often wondered what had happened to her.

4. Turn one of the independent clauses into a dependent clause.

CORRECTED

No one saw the van *that the bank robbers drove to Mexico.*

Because the movie was so exciting, we discussed it on the way home.

Tom, *who never saw Alice again,* often wondered what had happened to her.

4.1 Sentence Fragments

■ *Identify the following as complete sentences (c) or as fragments (f).*

EXAMPLES

We love to eat at Tony's. _____ *c* _____

Because his pizzas have thicker crusts. _____ *f* _____

1. Priced at $12.00 each. _____

   Ballpoint pens were first marketed in 1945. _____

2. When potatoes first appeared in Europe during

   the 1600s. _____

   They were believed to cause venereal disease. _____

3. Looming high above quiet valleys. _____

   Cader Idris, one of the highest peaks in Wales. _____

4. Ken Griffey Jr. and Ken Griffey Sr. made baseball

   history in 1990. _____

   As the only father and son to hit back-to-back

   home runs in a major league game. _____

5. The fiftieth anniversary of the Normandy Invasion.

   It brought back painful memories for many. _____

6. Many people enjoy gardening. _____

   Because they like to work outdoors. _____

7. The first baseball game ever televised was in Tokyo,

   Japan. _____

   Not in the United States. _____

8. She loves tandoori chicken. _____

He is a vegetarian. _____

9. The children were a little scared. _____

Although none of them admitted it. _____

10. In the first draft of the Declaration of Independence. _____

Was a clause abolishing slavery in the colonies. _____

11. Thomas Edison is America's most important inventor. _____

Holding over 1,300 patents in the United States

and abroad. _____

12. Most gas grills come with permanent briquettes. _____

This makes them easier to use. _____

13. Being more independent and less trouble to care for. _____

Cats have now surpassed dogs as America's most

popular pet. _____

14. Laptop computers often weigh less than five pounds. _____

Many feature hard disks. _____

15. Even in an age of film. _____

Children's theater is growing in popularity. _____

16. Foods such as Greek bread, Chinese *jai,* and Italian

roast chicken. _____

Religious significance for some people. _____

17. In both sales and assets. _____

The largest industrial corporation in the United

States is General Motors. _____

18. The first woman member of the United States
Senate was Rebecca Latimer Felton of Georgia.   _____

She was appointed in 1922.   _____

19. *The Pelican Brief,* a movie starring Denzel
Washington and Julia Roberts.   _____

Was based on the novel by John Grisham.   _____

20. Over the past decade, but during the last several
years in particular.   _____

Spain has been the European leader in tourism.   _____

NAME _____

DATE _____ SCORE _____

4.2 Sentence Fragments

■ *Identify the following as complete sentences (c) or as fragments (f).*

1. _____ More American women participate in sports today than ever before.

2. _____ In the early 1970s, only four girls in a hundred played a high school sport.

3. _____ By the late 1990s, more than thirty girls in a hundred.

4. _____ Even more surprisingly, over half of the girls between ages twelve and sixteen played basketball.

5. _____ Less surprising is the number of women now playing sports professionally.

6. _____ Furthermore, because they have participated in high school sports.

7. _____ Women now attend more sporting events featuring female athletes.

8. _____ In fact, seven out of ten fans at WNBA games are women.

9. _____ A much higher percentage than attend NBA games.

10. _____ As more fans come to watch them, professional female athletes' salaries will increase.

11. _____ Not to mention their power to attract lucrative product endorsements.

12. _____ These financial incentives are certain to increase the number of

amateur and professional women athletes in the future.

Adapted from Jean Strouse, "She Got Game," *New Yorker,* 16 August 1999,
36–40.

4.3 Sentence Fragments

■ *Correct the following sentence fragments by joining them to the complete sentences.*

EXAMPLES
After driving all night and part of the morning, we finally neared the outskirts of Denver.
After the sun went down, the whippoorwills began their songs.

1. Although light usually travels about 186,000 miles per second. Scientists have slowed it down to 38 miles per hour.

2. The island of Britain actually contains three different countries. Those being England, Scotland, and Wales.

3. Students often don't know how to use punctuation marks effectively. Like the colon, the semicolon, and the dash.

4. Because it lies below the level of the Mississippi River. The city of New Orleans depends heavily on levees.

5. Standing 550 feet tall, the Washington Monument was the highest structure in the world. When it was completed in 1884.

6. Still visible after centuries of use and neglect. Roman roads can be traced in many parts of Europe today.

7. DNA testing, which has been used to analyze certain kinds of evidence in criminal cases. This procedure can be both useful and controversial.

8. Some states do not require residents to pay state income taxes. Florida being one example.

9. Originally, frankfurters contained beef. Whereas wieners contained veal and pork.

10. Country-western music is now more popular than any other musical style. Even more popular than the rock music that began in the 1950s.

11. The first transatlantic cable linked American and Europe in 1886. Which improved communication between the two continents immensely.

12. Although a popular breed in America. Angus cattle originated in Scotland.

13. Highway 1 runs down the California coast. Connecting such well-known cities as San Francisco, Monterey, and Los Angeles.

14. Unlike most rivers in North America, the Shenandoah River flows north. And empties into the Potomac.

15. Being the true founders of modern science. The ancient Greeks first advanced the idea that matter is made of tiny particles called atoms.

16. Probably about to drift even lower. Prices for portable compact disc players are very reasonable.

17. The state of Alaska has over 100,000 glaciers. Most of which are visible only from the air.

18. Seaweed in various forms is a popular food in certain countries. Such as Japan.

19. John Coltrane was a famous jazz musician of the 1950s and 1960s. Who helped popularize the soprano saxophone as a jazz instrument.

20. One of the oldest species living today. Crocodiles have inhabited the earth for over 100 million years.

NAME _____

DATE _____ SCORE _____

4.4 Comma Splices and Fused Sentences

Comma splices and fused sentences can be corrected in five principal ways:

1. Use a period and write two separate sentences.
2. Use a semicolon between two independent clauses.
3. Use a comma and a coordinating conjunction between two independent clauses.
4. Make one of the clauses dependent.
5. Make one of the clauses a phrase.

■ *In the blanks provided, indicate whether each of the following is a fused sentence* (fs) *or a comma splice* (cs)*; then correct the sentence on the worksheet. Identify the method you used by writing one of the five previously mentioned numbers in the blank.*

EXAMPLES

Kansas City calls itself the city of Fountains its goal is to build a new public fountain every year. _____cs-2_____

Death Valley, California, is now a desert it once was a large lake. _____fs-3_____

Albany is the capital of New York it is not the largest city. _____cs-4_____

1. Many think popcorn is a typical American food, it was also a favorite food in ancient times. _____

2. The clarinet is a popular woodwind instrument, it was invented about 1700. _____

3. Black troops fought in many battles during the Civil War, twenty-two soldiers won the Medal of Honor. _____

4. The English Channel Tunnel was designed to handle both rail and highway traffic, it has been nicknamed the "Chunnel." _____

5. The Appalachian Trail is popular with hikers it runs from Georgia to Maine. _____

6. Rome destroyed Carthage in 146 B.C. it occupied Egypt in A.D. 30. _____

7. Some comets orbit the earth every few years, however others take thousands of years to circle the sun. _____

8. In 1854 Commodore Matthew Perry persuaded the Japanese to open their borders, that country had been closed to foreigners for centuries. _____

9. Shopping malls have transformed American cities and towns, they have taken the place of the ancient bazaar. _____

10. Many farmers find sunflowers to be a profitable crop they sell their seeds for birdfeed. _____

11. Many consider quilting to be a legitimate form of art it is practiced widely in the Appalachian region of the southeastern United States. _____

12. Colorado has five scenic historic highways, they wind through mountains, deserts, and forests. _____

13. High-frequency sound waves have many medical applications, one is to determine the health and even the gender of a fetus in the womb. _____

14. Medical science has extended life expectancy, consequently people need to develop hobbies that can provide meaningful activities in retirement. _____

15. The highest civilian award by the government of the United States is the Presidential Medal of Freedom, the award was established in 1963 by President John F. Kennedy. _____

16. High-definition televisions produce very clear pictures, furthermore they also produce the clear sound of a compact disc. _____

17. Cowrie shells may be found in tourist shops near beach resorts, they were once used as money in many parts of the world. _____

18. Some tides change approximately every twelve hours the moon is the cause of these massive shifts of ocean water. _____

19. John Keats and Stephen Crane have something in common, both writers died of tuberculosis while they were still in their twenties. _____

20. The USS *Constitution* was launched in 1797, it is still in commission. _____

4.5 Sentence Fragments, Comma Splices, and Fused Sentences: Review 1

■ *Revise the following paragraph to eliminate sentence fragments, comma splices, and fused sentences. As you revise, be sure to change capitalization and to add conjunctions as well as to correct punctuation.*

Computer networks have become a very popular part of the information superhighway, on the Internet, for example, users can send messages almost instantaneously to anyone on the network anywhere in the world. This form of interpersonal electronic communication is often called email, it is much faster and often less expensive than traditional postal systems. Internet users with similar interests have formed thousands of electronic discussion groups on the Internet, they share ideas and exchange information by posting messages on electronic bulletin boards. Many of these groups are scholarly in nature, many more are very informal some are even considered trivial. Many magazines and newspapers now publish electronic editions, Internet users can subscribe to them electronically. Having information about current affairs, sports, weather, books, movies, music, and many other subjects delivered electronically to their computer screens instead of to their mailboxes.

NAME _____

DATE _____ SCORE _____

4.6 Sentence Fragments, Comma Splices, and Fused Sentences: Review 2

■ *Revise the following paragraph to eliminate sentence fragments, comma splices, and fused sentences. As you revise, be sure to change capitalization and to add conjunctions as well as to correct punctuation.*

The original model for Dracula was Vlad the Impaler. A fifteenth-century warrior prince of Walachia in eastern Europe. According to Romanian legend, the sadistic Prince Vlad took his meals amid a forest of impaled, groaning victims after each course Vlad washed down his food with his victim's blood. In the belief that it imbued him with supernatural strength. Vlad's crimes were legend imprisoned himself, he tortured mice and birds for amusement. His mountaintop retreat, known as Castle Drakula. Suggested the name of the vampire villain of novel and film fame.

Adapted from Charles Panati, *Extraordinary Origins of Everyday Things*
(New York: Harper, 1987), 179–180.

4.7 Sentence Fragments, Comma Splices, and Fused Sentences: Review 3

■ *Revise the following paragraph to eliminate sentence fragments, comma splices, and fused sentences. As you revise, be sure to change capitalization and to add conjunctions as well as to correct punctuation.*

Although turquoise was mined by Egyptian pharaohs over five thousand years ago and traded by Chinese emperors for centuries. Most Americans associate this beautiful stone with their own desert southwest. For good reason. Over a thousand years ago, ancient Mayans were importing turquoise from what is now New Mexico. The mines were surprisingly large, archaeologists estimate that Native American miners dug thousands of tons of rock. Fewer than twenty active mines are in this country today, however, most of the turquoise dug now comes from China.

Adapted from Joseph Harris, "Tantalizing Turquoise,"
Smithsonian 30, no. 5 (1999): 70–80.

5   Verb Forms

VERBS

All verbs have three principal parts:

> the **infinitive** (*to concern*)
>
> the **past tense** (*concerned*)
>
> the **past participle** (*concerned*)

Regular, Irregular Verbs

Verbs can be regular or irregular in form. **Regular verbs** (*add, help*) form the past tense and the past participle by adding *-d, -ed,* or sometimes *-t (kept, dreamt).* The principal parts of *add* and *help* are *add, added, added; help, helped, helped.*

    Irregular verbs change form in the past tense and the past participle. Some irregular verbs (*begin, sing*) form the past tense and the past participle by changing a single vowel (*sing, sang, sung*). Other irregular verbs change more than one letter (*drive, drove, driven*). The principal parts of irregular verbs are listed in the dictionary. If these parts are not listed, you can assume that the verb is regular.

Transitive, Intransitive Verbs

Verbs also can be **transitive** (take a direct object) or **intransitive** (do not take a direct object).

TRANSITIVE VERB
> The cook *tasted* the special *sauce*. [*Sauce* is the direct object.]

INTRANSITIVE VERB
> The rain fell on the roof. [*Fell* does not take a direct object.]

    Especially troublesome are the irregular verbs *lie, lay; sit, set; rise, raise.* The verbs *lay, set,* and *raise* are transitive and take a direct object. The verbs *lie, sit,* and *rise* are intransitive and do not take a direct object.

    Each of these verbs has a specific meaning. *Lie* means to recline or to be situated; *lay,* to place. *Sit* means to be seated; *set,* to place or arrange. *Rise* means to get up; *raise* means to lift. When trying to decide on the correct form of the verb, think of the meaning you want, whether the verb takes a direct object, the tense you need, and the correct principal part. (See also pp. 82–83.)

EXAMPLES OF TROUBLESOME VERBS USED CORRECTLY

She *lays* the book on the table. [present tense of *lay*]

She *laid* the book on the table and left. [past tense of *lay*]

The boat *lies* in the harbor. [present tense of *lie*]

The boat *lay* in the harbor most of last week. [past tense of *lie*]

The waiter *set* the plate on the table. [*Plate* is the direct object.]

The archaeologist *laid* the relics taken from the temple on the examining table. [*Relics* is the direct object.]

The honor guard will *raise* the flag. [*Flag* is the direct object.]

Some of the swimmers were *lying* on the beach. [*Lying* is intransitive and takes no object.]

The sewing basket was *sitting* in the corner. [*Sitting* is intransitive and takes no object.]

The speaker *rises* to address the meeting. [*Rises* is intransitive and takes no object.]

The principal parts of these verbs are included in the following list of difficult verbs.

Principal Parts of Some Troublesome Verbs

INFINITIVE	PAST TENSE	PAST PARTICIPLE
arise	arose	arisen
awake	awoke, awaked	awoken, awaked
be	was	been
bear (to carry)	bore	borne
bear (to give birth)	bore	born, borne
begin	began	begun
bid (offer)	bid	bid
bid (order or say)	bade	bidden
bite	bit	bitten, bit
blow	blew	blown
break	broke	broken
bring	brought	brought
burst	burst	burst
choose	chose	chosen
come	came	come
deal	dealt	dealt
dig	dug	dug
dive	dived, dove	dived
do	did	done
drag	dragged	dragged
draw	drew	drawn
dream	dreamed, dreamt	dreamed, dreamt
drink	drank	drunk
drive	drove	driven
drown	drowned	drowned
eat	ate	eaten
fall	fell	fallen
find	found	found
flee	fled	fled

INFINITIVE	PAST TENSE	PAST PARTICIPLE
fly	flew	flown
forget	forgot	forgotten, forgot
freeze	froze	frozen
get	got	gotten, got
give	gave	given
go	went	gone
grow	grew	grown
hang (to execute)	hanged	hanged
hang (to suspend)	hung	hung
have	had	had
hear	heard	heard
know	knew	known
lay	laid	laid
lead	led	led
lend	lent	lent
let	let	let
lie	lay	lain
light	lighted, lit	lighted, lit
lose	lost	lost
pay	paid	paid
pay (rope)	payed	payed
plead	pleaded, pled	pleaded, pled
prove	proved	proven, proved
raise	raised	raised
ride	rode	ridden
ring	rang, rung	rung
rise	rose	risen
run	ran	run
say	said	said
see	saw	seen
set	set	set
shine (to give light)	shone	shone
shine (to polish)	shined	shined
show	showed	shown, showed
shrink	shrank, shrunk	shrunk
sing	sang, sung	sung
sink	sank, sunk	sunk
sit	sat	sat
slide	slid	slid
sow	sowed	sown, sowed
speak	spoke	spoken
spit	spit, spat	spit, spat
spring	sprang, sprung	sprung
stand	stood	stood
steal	stole	stolen
stink	stank, stunk	stunk
suppose	supposed	supposed
swim	swam, swum	swum
swing	swung	swung
take	took	taken
tear	tore	torn
use	used	used

TENSE AND SEQUENCE OF TENSES

Use verbs carefully to express distinctions of time. Avoid needless shifts of tense.

Usually the **present tense** expresses present time.

> The architect *is designing* a new office complex.

It also may show repeated action.

> The architect *designs* office complexes.

The **past tense** shows past time.

> The architect *designed* a new office complex.
>
> I *lay* in the sun for an hour. [past tense of verb *lie*]

The **future tense** shows future time.

> I *shall go* home for lunch.

Perfect Tenses

The three perfect tenses are used in well-defined sequences. They indicate time or action completed before another time or action.

1. Use **present perfect** with present.

   > I *have asked* her to help, and she *refuses*.

2. Use **past perfect** with past.

   > He *had wanted* to diet, but he *could* not.

3. Use **future perfect** with future.

   > He *will have finished* before we *will begin*.

Infinitive

An infinitive usually takes the present tense when it expresses action that occurs at the same time as that of the controlling verb.

> I *desired* to leave.
>
> To *complete* the project, we *had* to work overtime yesterday.

Relationships between verbs should be logical and consistent.

Inconsistencies in tense confuse readers by blurring time distinctions.

CONFUSING

After John *left* the theater, he *goes* to the restaurant for dinner. [past action or repeated action?]

CLEAR

After John *left* the theater, he *went* to the restaurant for dinner. [past action]

VOICE

When the subject of the sentence acts, the verb is in the active voice.

We *will complete* the sales report before Wednesday. [We act.]

When the subject is acted upon, the verb is in the passive voice.

The sales report *will be completed* before Wednesday. [The report is acted upon.]

Because sentences in the passive voice always require both a form of the verb *to be* and a past participle of another verb and sometimes omit the doer of the action, unnecessary use of passive voice can be both wordy and confusing.

WORDY

Cleaning of the cafeteria tables should be done by student workers.

CONCISE

Student workers should clean the cafeteria tables.

CONFUSING

Some errors were made. [by whom or what?]

CLEAR

We made some errors.

SUBJUNCTIVE MOOD

Use the subjunctive mood to show wishes, commands, or conditions contrary to fact.

I wish I *were* rich. [wish]

The rules require that we *be* silent. [command]

If I *were* vacationing this week, I would be a happy person. [condition contrary to fact]

5.1 Verb Forms

- *Circle the correct verb form. Remember that intransitive verbs do not take direct objects. Remember that transitive verbs do take direct objects. Look for both the meaning and the tense of the verb.*

EXAMPLES

I cannot remember where I (lay, (laid)) my grocery list. [The verb *laid,* the past tense of *lay,* is transitive and takes the direct object *list.*]

The wind has (rose, (risen)) and the leaves have (flew, (flown)) everywhere. [*Risen* and *flown* are intransitive; they have no direct objects.]

How many pancakes have you (ate, (eaten))?

1. The lazy dog (lay, laid) on the sun-dappled porch for hours.

2. The shipwrecked sailors had not (ate, eaten) for days when their rescuers finally arrived.

3. The investigator was (suppose, supposed) to report to his supervisor five days after he completed his work.

4. Many tourists have (ask, asked) about the best restaurants in London, Paris, and Madrid.

5. The Gilbert Stuart portraits of George and Martha Washington were (hung, hanged) in the Boston Athenaeum.

6. The fruiterer (set, sat) her best wares on the table first.

7. According to Homer's *Iliad,* Achilles (dragged, drug) Hector's corpse behind his chariot.

8. Home gardeners have (develop, developed) many different varieties of day lilies.

9. During the hurricane the coastal roads were (tore, torn) up by huge waves and high tides.

10. Hungry and exhausted, the fortress's weary defenders (rose, raised) the white flag of surrender.

NAME _____

DATE _____ SCORE _____

5.2 Verb Forms

■ *Circle the correct verb form.*

EXAMPLE

It (taken, (took)) her several years to achieve her career goal.

1. Catching the terrified faces of each figure, Goya (froze, frozed) a brutal moment in his country's history in a memorable painting.

2. The racing team (raised, rose) the yacht's sail and turned it into the wind.

3. During the presidential election campaign of 1952, several dissenting groups (breaked, broke) from the Democratic Party.

4. Palm oil has been (use, used) to make everything from cooking oil and ice cream to hand soap and shoe polish.

5. The job applicant (set, sat) in the reception room waiting to be interviewed.

6. DVD technology has (began, begun) to change the way people view movies at home.

7. When the car's water hose (bursted, burst), the driver pulled to the side of the road.

8. No one wants to (loose, lose) the respect of her peers.

9. After being read his rights, the suspect was (lead, led) into police custody.

10. The frightened children had (laid, lain) awake all night.

5.3 Verb Forms

■ *Write the correct verb form in the space provided. Consult the list of troublesome verbs at the beginning of this chapter; then identify the correct verb form (infinitive, past tense, or past participle) in the space to the right.*

EXAMPLE
Most art students have __*prepared*__ (to prepare) a
portfolio by the time they graduate from college.   *past participle*

1. Before the grueling match ended, the tennis player

   must have _____ (to drink) three quarts

   of water.   _____

2. The sun had _____ (to set) long before

   the exhausted climbers returned to camp.   _____

3. Scientists have only _____ (to begin) to

   unlock the secrets of human DNA.   _____

4. After the concert was over, the diva confessed that

   she could not have _____ (to sing) an-

   other note.   _____

5. Well-preserved bodies of Ice Age animals have been

   discovered _____ (to freeze) in the Arctic

   tundra.   _____

6. The kindergartners _____ (to see) the

   popular movie twice last week.   _____

7. Pony express riders often covered seventy miles a

   day and _____ (to change) horses five or

   six times during a trip.   _____

8. There is a growing market for food supplements that

   are _____ (to suppose) to prevent or cure

   many common ailments.   _____

9. The new recruits were not _____ (to use)

   to the rigors of basic training.   _____

10. Two centuries ago, huge flocks of Carolina parakeets

    _____ (to darken) the skies all along the

    eastern seaboard.   _____

NAME _____

DATE _____ SCORE _____

5.4 Tense and Sequence of Tenses

Avoid needless shifts of tense. The **present tense** usually expresses present time or may show repeated action. The **past tense** shows past time. The **future tense** shows future time. The **perfect tenses** indicate time or action completed before another time or action.

■ *Correct the tense of the italicized verbs and verbals.*

EXAMPLES

City planners consider an area's economic needs and ~~will plan~~ *plan* zoning laws.

We left the cabin and ~~go~~ *went* for a walk.

1. After the tornado destroyed Robert's house, he *receives* a check from his insurance company.

2. Many fans had waited in line for hours before they *had received* tickets to the championship game.

3. Many people *ask* accountants for help with their income tax returns last year.

4. Before the end of this decade, the Internet *transformed* the way stocks are traded in America.

5. The Connecticut River, the longest waterway in New England, *has drained* an area of eleven thousand square miles as it flows from the Canadian border to Long Island Sound.

6. In the not-too-distant future, it may be possible for people to *have grown* new organs to replace diseased ones.

7. Offshore tornadoes, known as waterspouts, *were known* to drop large numbers of fish on inland communities from time to time.

8. Elephant herds haul away tons of silt from shallow water holes after their ritualistic herd baths; thus, they *cleaned* the water and *created* water holes for other animals.

9. Fossil remains found in Antarctica *had linked* that continent with South America and have provided further evidence that the two land masses were once connected.

10. The term *tailgate trombone* once referred to a New Orleans trombonist who *plays* while standing on the back of a horse-drawn parade cart.

5.5 Voice

Active voice is preferred to **passive voice** in writing. When the subject acts, the verb is in the active voice. When the subject is acted upon, the verb is in the passive voice.

■ *In the following sentences change the passive voice to active.*

EXAMPLES

Pride is instilled and friendships are promoted by voluntary neighborhood clean-up campaigns.

Voluntary neighborhood clean-up campaigns instill pride and promote friendships.

[*instilled* and *promoted* changed to action forms *instill* and *promote* with direct objects *pride* and *friendships*]

1. The first telephone conversation was held between Alexander Graham Bell and Thomas A. Watson on March 10, 1876.

   _____

   _____

2. Over one thousand people lost their lives when the *Lusitania,* a British steamer, was torpedoed by a German submarine on May 7, 1915.

   _____

   _____

3. A French army under Philip VI was defeated by English archers at the Battle of Crécy, the first important battle of the Hundred Years' War.

   _____

   _____

4. Plimouth Plantation, a re-creation of the Pilgrims' first settlement in America, is visited by thousands of tourists each year.

   _____

   _____

5. The presence of water on the moon has been revealed by satellite photographs.

_____

_____

6. Potential jurors were asked by the defense attorney to state their opinions on the death penalty.

_____

_____

7. As much as 400 inches of rain per year is received by some Hawaiian islands.

_____

_____

8. Unattended luggage is viewed very suspiciously by the authorities at international airports.

_____

_____

9. Maple syrup was produced by Native Americans long before French and English explorers came to North America.

_____

_____

10. Malaria, a debilitating and sometimes fatal disease, can be cured by doctors.

_____

_____

5.6 Verb Forms: Review

■ *Revise the following paragraph, correcting all errors in verb tense and verb form.*

Ancient Greece produce many great political leaders, historians, philoso-

phers, and scientists. Alexander the Great had spread Greek culture all the

way to India. Herodotus writes the first historical work of Western civiliza-

tion. Socrates, who never actually has written anything, nevertheless had a

profound influence on future philosophers. Aristotle has given to the mod-

ern world biological classifications and a scientific approach that is requir-

ing all theory to be base on observed facts. These great thinkers not only

shape our past; they will have continued to influence our future.

6   Subject and Verb: Agreement

Use singular verbs with singular subjects, and use plural verbs with plural subjects. The *-s* or *-es* ending of the present tense of a verb in the third person (*he hopes, she stops*) indicates the singular. For most nouns, however, these same endings indicate the plural.

After Compound Subject

A compound subject with *and* usually takes a plural verb.

> Quiltwork *and* other traditional handicrafts *are* now considered folk art.

When compound subjects are joined by *or, either . . . or,* or *neither . . . nor,* the verb should agree with the subject closest to it.

> Neither the diagram nor the directions are easy to read.
> Neither the directions nor the diagram is easy to read.

Collective Nouns

Collective nouns (words like *family, flock,* and *jury*) take a singular verb when referring to a group as a unit; they take a plural verb when the members of a group are treated individually.

> My *family is* going on a trip this weekend.
> My *family are* going to Hawaii, New Jersey, and Ohio on Labor Day.

After Relative Pronoun

After a relative pronoun (such as *who, which,* and *that*), the verb in the relative clause has the same person and number as the *antecedent* of the pronoun.

> Over half the people who *work* in retail sales are women.

After Titles

A title of a book or film is singular and requires a singular verb, even if it contains plural words and ideas.

> *Elements of Films* is a useful book.

After *There, Here*

In sentences that begin with *there* and *here,* the verb agrees with the subject of the sentence.

> There *is* an old *mill* on this road. [*Mill* is the subject.]
>
> There *are* many *challenges* in this project. [*Challenges* is the subject.]

Word Groups

Word groups such as the prepositions *in addition to* and *as well as* do not change the number of the subject when they separate the subject and the verb.

> The *mayor as well as* state officials *is* examining the problem.

The Subject

The subject of the sentence, not the predicate nominative, determines the number of the verb.

> His main *strength is* his abilities to listen and to follow instructions.

When the subject in a sentence is *inverted,* the verb should agree with the *subject* of the sentence, not with the word that comes directly before the verb.

> At the party *were Beatrice* and her *sister.* [Plural verb agrees with compound subject.]

6.1 Subject and Verb Agreement

■ *Underline each subject once; then write the correct verb in the blank at the right.*

EXAMPLES

Local banks and chambers of commerce usually (provide, provides) useful information to new residents.

provide

Neither the team members nor their coach (expect, expects) a victory.

expects

1. There are more than 250 tributaries that (empties, empty) into the Mississippi River.

    _____

2. Visiting national parks and driving through small towns that are off main highways (is, are) favorite types of vacations for many people.

    _____

3. A relief party of eight volunteers (was, were) sent to rescue the stranded skiers.

    _____

4. Not everyone who lives in our neighborhood (attends, attend) the same school.

    _____

5. Several dignitaries as well as the governor (was, were) invited to visit the new hospital.

    _____

6. Copper is one of the few minerals that (appears, appear) in a pure form in nature.

    _____

7. There (is, are) several different types of audiocassette tapes that consumers may purchase.

    _____

8. Indiana as well as Wisconsin, Illinois, and Michigan (touches, touch) Lake Michigan.

    _____

9. Not only gold but also silver, lead, copper, manganese, and arsenic (is, are) found in the mountains of Montana.

    _____

10. Whoever (says, say) finding a parking place on campus is easy has never tried to park during peak hours.

    _____

11. Members of the university's ice hockey club, which (competes, compete) against teams from across the state, buy their own equipment. _____

12. On the guest list for the private wedding (was, were) a famous comedian and two television stars. _____

13. The audience, which included people of different ethnic groups, (was, were) deeply offended by the speaker's remarks. _____

14. The stress of professional competition, not to mention a serious knee injury, (has, have) convinced her to retire. _____

15. Orlando's taste in music and art (tends, tend) to be more contemporary than classical. _____

6.2 Subject and Verb Agreement

■ *Correct the errors in subject and verb agreement in the following paragraph.*

Although many people go a lifetime without seeing one, meteorites hit the earth's atmosphere with surprising frequency and sometimes strikes its surface with catastrophic effect. There is, according to scientists, ten major meteor showers per year. Average citizens as well as the most dedicated scientist is most likely to see a meteor during one of these times. The meteorites that fall in these showers are tiny—about the size of a grain of sand—and are visible for only a few seconds. Much larger meteorites, however, has penetrated the atmosphere and struck the earth. The Willamette meteorite, discovered in Oregon, weighs over fifteen tons, and both the Almighito meteorite and the Hoba West meteorite weighs twice that much. In the 1950s, scientists discovered a depression in Canada that is over four hundred miles across. This huge crater may have been formed by the largest meteorite ever to strike the earth's surface.

7 Pronouns: Agreement, Reference, and Usage

ANTECEDENTS

An antecedent is a noun or pronoun to which a following pronoun refers. Use singular pronouns to refer to singular antecedents, and use plural pronouns to refer to plural antecedents. Use a plural pronoun to refer to compound antecedents except in those cases in which the antecedents refer to the same person.

> *Phyllis* asked the waiter to bring *her* check. [Singular pronoun *her* refers to singular antecedent *Phyllis*.]
>
> *We* asked the waiter to bring *our* checks. [Plural pronoun *our* refers to plural antecedent *We*.]
>
> Last week *my first cousin and best friend* reported the news of *her* promotion. [Singular pronoun *her* refers to *cousin* and to *friend*.]

When referring to people, use *who;* when referring to animals or to things, use *which* or *that*.

> The horse *that* escaped was an expensive thoroughbred.
>
> The senator *who* wrote the bill lost the next election.

Avoid using pronouns that refer vaguely to entire sentences or to unidentified people.

VAGUE

> I have trouble taking standardized tests. *This* is my problem. [*This* is vague—what is the antecedent?]
>
> *You* know that *they* will do *it* every time. [*You, they,* and *it* are vague references—to whom or to what, specifically, do they refer?]

Make sure pronouns refer clearly to only one antecedent.

UNCERTAIN

> Jack went to the doctor after he returned from vacation. [Does *he* refer to *Jack* or to *doctor?*]

CLEAR

> After Jack returned from vacation, he went to the doctor. [*He* now clearly refers only to *Jack*.]

7.1 Pronouns: Agreement and Reference

A pronoun is a word that stands for a noun. Use singular pronouns to refer to singular nouns; use plural pronouns to refer to plural nouns.

■ *In the following sentences choose the correct pronouns and write them in the blanks at the right.*

EXAMPLES

The band dedicated the song to all (its, their) fans.

_____*its*_____

County maps are useful for census takers as (they, he or she) attempt to reach all households.

_____*they*_____

1. Many insects and other animals use protective coloration to confuse, intimidate, or hide from (its, their) enemies.

_____

2. Freight trains were called "rattlers" in the 1840s because (it, they) made so much noise.

_____

3. In 1917, the French executed Dutch dancer Gertrud Margarete Zelle, (who, which) was better known as Mata Hari, because they were convinced she was spying for the Germans.

_____

4. The oil company raised (its, their) prices soon after the embargo was announced.

_____

5. The pintail duck is found throughout the United States and the Caribbean, but (it, they) usually nests in Alaska and Canada.

_____

6. Problems with (their, its) accounting procedures kept the company from winning government contracts.

_____

7. Thomas Edison invented the phonograph in 1877, and from then until the 1970s (it, they) supported popular music.

_____

8. People (who, which) fear heights suffer from acrophobia.

_____

9. My roommate and her sister found (herself, themselves) lost in Paris without luggage, money, or
   passports.   _____

10. Many researchers are now studying the causes of
    heart failure to find ways to prevent (it, them).   _____

7.2 Pronouns: Agreement and Reference

■ *Revise the following sentences to improve pronoun agreement and reference. Write C in the blank at the right by any sentence that is correct.*

EXAMPLE

Original: All of the law students submitted his or her reports today.

Correction: All of the law students submitted their reports today.

1. When the temperature is more than ninety degrees, they can quickly dehydrate anyone working or playing outdoors. _____

2. A dissatisfied customer will often tell their friends about a bad experience. _____

3. Some singers overestimate their musical range, and this miscalculation causes them to strain their vocal cords. _____

4. The committee submitted its revised budget last week. _____

5. The well drillers finally found water at seven hundred feet, the greatest depth it had ever had to drill. _____

6. Insurance rates continue to climb, and this is why some people choose not to own a car. _____

7. A busy executive must find time to pursue one of their hobbies or outside interests. _____

8. College seniors often worry about what he or she will do after graduation. _____

9. Children are sometimes surprised to find that his or her role in the family changes as time passes. _____

10. The supervisor asked everyone on the morning shift to turn in his or her vacation request by noon. _____

8 Pronouns: Case

Case refers to the role a noun or pronoun plays in a sentence. Case shows whether a noun or pronoun is functioning as a subject, an object, or a possessor. Accordingly, pronouns have three cases: subjective, possessive, and objective. Personal pronouns and the relative pronoun *who* change in form to indicate these cases.

> Subjective (acting)—I, you, he, she, it, we, they, who
>
> Possessive (possessing)—my (mine), your (yours), his, her (hers), its, our (ours), their (theirs), whose
>
> Objective (acted upon)—me, you, him, her, it, us, them, whom

To determine case, find out how a word is used in its own clause—for example, whether it is a subject, a subjective complement, a possessive, or an object.

Use the **subjective case** for subjects and subjective complements.

SUBJECT
> The contractor and *I* are about to reach an agreement. [Use *I,* not *me,* for the subject.]

SUBJECTIVE COMPLEMENT (OR PREDICATE NOMINATIVE)
> The winner was *I*. [Use *I,* not *me,* after a linking verb.]

Use the **possessive case** to show ownership and with gerunds.

> *Their work* was complete. [ownership]
>
> *His* constant *whistling* annoys his coworkers. [gerund]

The possessive forms of personal pronouns (including the pronoun *its*) do *not* have apostrophes.

> *Hers* is the best solution.
>
> *Its* handle is broken.

The possessive forms of indefinite pronouns (*everybody's, one's, anyone's*) do have apostrophes. Contractions such as *it's* (for *it is*) and *she's* (for *she is*) do have apostrophes.

Use the **objective case** for the object of a preposition and for the subject of an infinitive.

> Who among *us* will volunteer? [*Us* is the object of *among.*]
>
> The college selected *her* to be the coach. [*Her* is the subject of the infinitive *to be.*]

For Interrogative Pronouns

The case of interrogatives (*who, whose, whom, what, which* used in questions) depends on their use in specific clauses.

> Whom did you call about our new book orders? [Use *whom*, not *who*, because the interrogative pronoun is a direct object of *call*.]

Appositives

For pronouns used as appositives (words that rename nouns or pronouns) use the same case as the noun or pronoun renamed.

SUBJECTIVE

> Only we—Sharon and I—were excused. [*Sharon* and *I* rename the subject *we*; hence, use *I*, not *me*.]

OBJECTIVE

> The instructor excused two of us—Sharon and me. [*Sharon* and *me* rename the object of the preposition *of*; hence, use the objective case.]

After *Than* or *As*

The correct case of a pronoun used after *than* or *as* is determined by completing the missing verb of the clause:

> Margaret is taller than I. [*Than I am* is the complete clause; *I* is the subject of the clause.]
>
> She worked harder than you or I. [*than you or I worked*]
>
> This crisis hurt him more than her. [*more than it hurt her*; *her* is the object]

NAME _____

DATE _____ SCORE _____

8.1 Pronoun Case

■ *In the following sentences choose the correct case forms and write them in the blanks.*

EXAMPLES

(Whoever, Whomever) invented the wheel deserves the gratitude of everyone.

Whoever

[subject of verb *invented*]

About (whom, who) are you speaking?

whom

[object of preposition *about*]

1. Joseph Haydn was an Austrian composer (who, whom) developed the sonata form.

_____

2. David and (she, her) enjoy hiking in the Grand Tetons.

_____

3. We plan to visit Margaret and (he, him) after Memorial Day.

_____

4. Herbert Hoover's mother, a traveling Quaker preacher, died when he was eight, leaving (he, him) and his brother as orphans.

_____

5. The race was nearly a tie, and (who, whom) won it was difficult to determine.

_____

6. The sales clerk gave (we, us) coupons worth three dollars.

_____

7. Who knows our family better than (we, us)?

_____

8. Several senators excused (theirselves, themselves) from the meeting.

_____

9. The store manager knew (her, she) to be completely trustworthy.

_____

10. The Agent-of-the-Month award goes to (whoever, whomever) sells property worth the greatest amount, not (whoever, whomever) sells the most pieces of property.

_____

8.2 Pronoun Case

■ *In the following sentences choose the correct case forms and write them in the blanks.*

EXAMPLE
(Their, Them) singing is delightful.

Their

[possessive case with gerund]

1. I had heard about (you, your) moving to a new neighborhood, but no one could tell me your new address.

_____

2. It was (he, him) who first proposed a change in office procedures.

_____

3. Neither we nor (they, them) could recall the third labor of Hercules.

_____

4. A bases-loaded double in the ninth inning brought Teneka and (I, me) to our feet.

_____

5. "To (who, whom) should I write this check?" she asked the antiques dealer.

_____

6. (Who, Whom) did the publisher decide to choose as the new editor?

_____

7. No one knew (who, whom) would replace the retiring attorney general.

_____

8. No one works harder than (they, them), but no one seems to enjoy his or her work more.

_____

9. The tennis league gave trophies to Jasmine and (I, me).

_____

10. (Whoever, Whomever) has the key to the garage should return it immediately.

_____

8.3 Pronoun Case and Agreement: Review 1

■ *Revise the following paragraph, correcting all errors in pronoun case and agreement.*

When Henry Hudson's crew mutinied in 1611, setting he and eight others adrift in James Bay, they inaugurated a mystery that has never been solved. Today, nearly four hundred years later, the fate of this famous explorer is still unknown. Some believe Hudson may have sailed as far as Spitzburgen Island in the shallop, or small boat, that his crew left him. No one was more determined than him, but him and his companions almost certainly did not travel that far. In 1668, an American explorer told stories of an English-style house near where the Rupert River empties into James Bay. Later explorers repeated stories, told by natives, of a group of Englishmen whom died on these desolate shores. If so, their graves have never been discovered. The mystery remains.

Adapted from Lawrence Millman, "Looking for Henry Hudson,"
Smithsonian 30, no. 7 (1999): 100–110.

8.4 Pronoun Case and Agreement: Review 2

■ *Revise the following paragraph, correcting all errors in pronoun case and agreement.*

The original fairy tale did not always end "happily ever after." They were often extremely violent. In the authentic version of "Little Red Riding Hood," for example, the wolf attacks and kills the little girl at the end of the story. Both her and her grandmother lose their lives. Offended by this violence, some nineteenth-century artists refused to illustrate the tale. It was them, not the publisher, who believed that a story for children should have a happier ending. One illustrator, who modern versions of the tale are indebted to, changed the tale. He introduced a hunter, whom appeared in time to save Red Riding Hood—and the tale.

Adapted from Charles Panati, *Extraordinary Origins of Everyday Things*
(New York: Harper, 1987), 168.

9 Adjectives and Adverbs

ADJECTIVES AND ADVERBS COMPARED

Adjectives modify nouns and pronouns. **Adverbs** modify verbs, adjectives, and other adverbs.

> The *bright* light hurt *our* eyes. [*The* and *bright* are adjectives modifying *light,* and *our* is a possessive adjective modifying *eyes.*]
>
> The news spread *quickly.* [*Quickly* is an adverb modifying *spread.*]

Many adverbs are formed by adding *-ly* to adjectives (*sudden, suddenly; hasty, hastily*). Only a few adjectives (*lovely* and *friendly,* for example) have this ending.

> We had an *easy* choice to make. [*Easy* is an adjective.]
>
> We made the choice *easily.* [*Easily* is an adverb.]
>
> He wore gloves made from *real* buckskin. [*Real* is an adjective modifying *buckskin.*]
>
> I left work *really* tired last night. [*Really* is an adverb modifying *tired.*]

Some adverbs do not end in *-ly* (for example, *late, soon,* and *well*).

> The bus will arrive *soon.* [*Soon* modifies *will arrive.*]
>
> We left the party *late.* [*Late* modifies *left.*]
>
> The presidency fit her *well.* [*Well* modifies *fit.*]

Some adverbs have two forms, one with *-ly* and one without (*closely, close* and *quickly, quick*).

> The Chevy stopped *close* to the curb. [*Close* modifies *stopped.*]
>
> The chemist watched the reaction *closely.* [*Closely* modifies *watched.*]
>
> Come *quick!* [*Quick* modifies *come.*]
>
> The deckhand *quickly* tossed the raft overboard. [*Quickly* modifies *tossed.*]

NOTE: Although using *quick* as an adverb is often acceptable in speech, it is only rarely acceptable in formal writing. When in doubt, use *quickly.*

Use a predicate adjective, not an adverb, after a linking verb (for example, *be, become, seem, look, appear, feel, sound, smell, taste*).

> The *laundry* is *dry.* [*Dry* describes *laundry.*]
>
> The *tire* looked *flat.* [*Flat* describes *tire.*]
>
> The *pie* smells *delicious.* [*Delicious* describes *pie.*]

The adjective *good* and the adverb *well* are frequently misused; be sure to use them correctly.

> The *pianist* was *good*. [The linking verb *was* calls for an adjective to modify *pianist*, so *good* should be used.]
>
> The *pianist* played *well*. [To modify the verb *played*, the adverb *well* should be used.]

COMPARATIVE AND SUPERLATIVE FORMS

When comparing only two things, use the **comparative form.** Add *-er* to form the comparative of most short modifiers. When comparing three or more things, use the **superlative form.** Add *-est* to form the superlative of most short modifiers.

> She is a very *fast* sprinter. [positive form; no comparison]
>
> She is a *faster* sprinter than her brother. [comparative form]
>
> She is the *fastest* sprinter in her conference. [superlative form]

The comparative and superlative forms of long modifiers—that is, modifiers with several syllables—use *more, most* or *less, least* before the modifier instead of ending in *-er* or *-est.*

> She is *more capable* than her sister. [not *capabler*]
>
> She is the *most capable* of her sisters. [not *capablest*]

Some adjectives and adverbs have irregular comparative and superlative forms.

> *good, better, best*
>
> *bad, worse, worst*
>
> *much, more, most*
>
> *little, less, least*

NOTE: Some adjectives imply an absolute state and cannot be intensified.

NOT

> Her designs are very unique.

BUT

> Her designs are unique.

9.1 Adjective or Adverb?

■ *Write the correct form of the adjective or adverb in the blank.*

EXAMPLES

The angry customer spoke (rapid, rapidly).   *rapidly*

[adverb *rapidly* modifying verb *spoke*]

(Slight, Slightly) sunlight is enough for this fern.   *Slight*

[adjective *slight* modifying noun *sunlight*]

1. The diva performed (capable, capably), but she did not inspire her listeners. _____

2. The nations of the British Commonwealth are not always tied (close, closely) to the British crown. _____

3. John Roebling worked (tireless, tirelessly) to complete the Brooklyn Bridge in 1883. _____

4. A statue of Vulcan stands (high, highly) over Birmingham, Alabama, as a symbol of that city's large steel industry. _____

5. Before the meetings began, the members of the trade commission from England were greeted very (warm, warmly). _____

6. The appraisers examined the silver coins (careful, carefully) before estimating their value. _____

7. Every applicant performed (good, well) on the tests. _____

8. The region of Brittany is (considerable, considerably) different from the rest of France. _____

9. The plain before the pioneers was (vast, vastly) and covered with wildflowers. _____

10. (Really, Real) good theater is almost always expensive to see. _____

11. Living History groups like the Society for Creative Anachronism pride themselves on how (good, well) they can re-create the costumes and weapons of the past.

_____

12. The townspeople rushed (frantic, frantically) to protect their homes from the fire.

_____

13. Many college students choose a major they hope will lead to a (good, well) paid job.

_____

14. Of my two sisters, Carmen is the (better, best) mathematician, but Linda is actually the (more, most) accurate accountant.

_____

15. The tropical storm developed very (quick, quickly) into a hurricane.

_____

16. The aroma of the freshly baked bread smelled (inviting, invitingly).

_____

17. Of the orchestra's eight violinists, she is clearly the (better, best).

_____

18. Although most outdoor thermometers performed very (good, well) in our tests, some did not register (accurate, accurately) in subfreezing weather.

_____

19. After studying for six hours, Tom was (real, really) ready to take a break.

_____

20. Today women (usual, usually) give birth in hospitals, but they did so only (infrequent, infrequently) a century ago.

_____

NAME _____

DATE _____ SCORE _____

9.2 Comparative and Superlative

The **comparative form** of the adjective or the adverb refers to two things; the **superlative form** refers to more than two things.

■ *Write the correct comparative or superlative form in the blanks.*

EXAMPLES

controversial   Boxing is probably the ___*most controversial*___ of all major sports.

funny   The comedian's latest routine is _____*funnier*_____ than his last one.

1. beneficial   Highly pigmented fruits and vegetables are _____ than many people realize.

2. little   Faster computers have made surfing the Internet _____ time-consuming than it once was.

3. serious   Reckless driving is a _____ traffic offense than is speeding.

4. visible   The northern lights are _____ in Alaska than in the forty-eight contiguous states.

5. tall   The _____ mountains in the Western Hemisphere are in the Andes.

6. great   Many baseball fans consider Babe Ruth the _____ hitter in the history of the sport.

7. good   Blueberries grow _____ in damp, acidic soils than in dry, alkaline soils.

8. small   The population of his hometown is _____ than the enrollment at many state universities.

9. good   Ty Cobb's batting average of .366 is still the _____ in the history of professional baseball.

10. long   If Norway's coastline were straight, it would stretch 12,500 miles, _____ than that of any other Scandinavian country.

   123

NAME _____

DATE _____ SCORE _____

9.3 Adjectives and Adverbs: Review

■ *Write a paragraph on a topic of your choice. Include at least five adjectives and five adverbs. Underline the adjectives once and the adverbs twice.*

_____

_____

_____

_____

_____

_____

_____

_____

_____

_____

_____

Sentence Structure

10 Coordination, Subordination, Completeness, Comparisons, and Consistency

COORDINATION

Linking a number of short independent clauses and sentences only with coordinating conjunctions produces wordiness and monotony; excessive coordination also fails to show precise relationships between thoughts.

EXCESSIVE COORDINATION

> The United States has changed significantly in the last fifty years, for the life expectancy of Americans has increased ten years for men and fifteen years for women, and the nation's work force has quadrupled.

IMPROVED

> The United States has changed significantly in the last fifty years. The life expectancy of Americans has increased ten years for men and fifteen years for women. In addition, the nation's work force has quadrupled.

SUBORDINATION

A **subordinate clause** is a group of words that contains both a subject and a predicate but cannot stand by itself as a sentence. Use subordinate clauses accurately and effectively to avoid excessive coordination and to achieve variety and proper emphasis. However, avoid excessive subordination, which results in long and monotonous sentences.

EXCESSIVE SUBORDINATION

> My grandfather took great pleasure throughout his life in the craft of carving wooden figures, which he learned to do when he was young, which was a time when people did not have the great number of amusements that we have today.

BETTER

> My grandfather, who lived in a time when people did not have the great number of amusements of today, learned when young to carve wooden figures. He took great pleasure in the craft throughout his life.

Express main ideas in independent clauses; express less important ideas in subordinate clauses.

IMPROPER SUBORDINATION

> Few people know that he got his seed from mills that made apple cider, although Johnny Appleseed became famous for planting apple trees throughout the Ohio Valley.

128

BETTER

Although few people know that he got his seed from mills that made apple cider, Johnny Appleseed became famous for planting apple trees throughout the Ohio Valley.

Avoid excessive overlapping of subordinate clauses. A series of clauses in which each one depends on the previous one is confusing.

OVERLAPPING SUBORDINATION

The United States Treasury Department, which is located in Washington, which is responsible for the printing and minting of currency, is also responsible for the protection of the president.

IMPROVED

Located in Washington, the United States Treasury Department is responsible for the printing and minting of currency and for the protection of the president.

COMPLETENESS

After *So, Such,* or *Too*

Make your sentences complete in structure and thought, especially sentences with *so, such,* or *too.*

NOT CLEAR

The storm was so violent. [So violent that what happened?]

CLEAR

The storm was so violent that we closed all the shutters.

NOT CLEAR

The secretary was too busy. [Too busy to do what?]

CLEAR

The secretary was too busy to answer the telephone.

Omission of Verbs and Prepositions

Do not omit a verb or a preposition that is necessary to the structure of the sentence.

NOT

We were interested and then bored by the lecture.

BUT

We were interested in and then bored by the lecture.

NOT

The passengers were impatient and the plane late.

BUT

The passengers were impatient, and the plane was late.

Omission of *That*

The omission of *that* is often confusing.

INCOMPLETE

He was grieved she did not love him.

COMPLETE

He was grieved that she did not love him.

COMPARISONS

Make comparisons clear and complete by comparing only similar terms, using the word *other* where necessary and avoiding awkward and incomplete comparisons.

INCORRECT

The bite of a person is often worse than a dog.

LOGICAL

The bite of a person is often worse than the bite of a dog.

INCORRECT

The Grand Canyon is larger than any canyon in the world.

LOGICAL

The Grand Canyon is larger than any other canyon in the world.

INCORRECT

Reading is one of the most pleasant if not the most pleasant pastimes one can enjoy. [After *one of the most pleasant,* the plural, *pastimes,* is required.]

BETTER

Reading is one of the most pleasant pastimes one can enjoy, if not the most pleasant.

OR

Reading is one of the most pleasant pastimes.

Avoid ambiguous comparisons.

AMBIGUOUS

We enjoyed visiting the city more than our parents. [*More* than visiting the parents, or *more* than the parents enjoyed visiting the city?]

CLEAR

We enjoyed visiting the city more than our parents did.

CONSISTENCY

Avoid confusing shifts in grammatical forms.

Shifts in Tense

INCORRECT

The doctor was well trained, but his patients are dissatisfied.

CORRECT

The doctor is well trained, but his patients are dissatisfied.

Shifts in Person

INCORRECT

When we flew over St. Louis, you could see the Mississippi River.

CORRECT

When we flew over St. Louis, we could see the Mississippi River.

Shifts in Number

INCORRECT

A person may decide on their vocation late in life.

CORRECT

People may decide on their vocations late in life.

Shifts in Voice

INCORRECT

The assignment *is read* by the student, and then she *answers* the questions at the end of the chapter.

CORRECT

The student *reads* the assignment, and then she *answers* the questions at the end of the chapter. [Put both parts of the sentence in the active voice.]

NAME _____

DATE _____ SCORE _____

10.1 Excessive Coordination

Sentences should be varied in length, structure, and emphasis. Coordination, subordination, parallelism, and word order should show relationships precisely and emphasize important elements of thought. Do not string together a number of short independent clauses; excessive coordination fails to show precise relationships between thoughts.

■ *Rewrite the following sentences to eliminate excessive coordination.*

EXAMPLE
The election results were close and both candidates declared victory, so the officials decided to recount the ballots.

Because the election results were close and both candidates
declared victory, the officials decided to recount the ballots.

1. The great masterpiece of Japanese literature is the *Tale of Genji,* and it was written during the Heian period (794–1185) by Lady Murasaki Shikibu; it was not translated into English until the twentieth century.

   _____

   _____

   _____

2. Millions of American teenagers take the SAT today, but this test was not developed until 1926, and it was not widely used until 1943.

   _____

   _____

   _____

3. Alice and her sisters are all scuba divers, so every year they meet at Marathon in the Florida Keys, and they spend a week there diving.

   _____

   _____

   _____

4. Internet companies are starting up at a record pace, and every type of business has been affected, but a shortage of qualified workers, office space, and advertising makes their success far from certain.

_____

_____

_____

5. The water cascaded over the falls, and we watched the salmon leaping into the air, and we wondered what compelled them to such struggle.

_____

_____

_____

6. The old-fashioned fairy tales were frightening, and they were intended to be, and children heard them and were likely to stay near home or on the path in the woods so the stories taught safety.

_____

_____

_____

7. Video games are big business, and much of their popularity is due to increasingly sophisticated graphics, but the best-selling video game in history is the hand-held Game Boy.

_____

_____

_____

8. Sunspots were discovered in the eighteenth century, and they have remained a mystery for two centuries, but now scientists are beginning to understand these solar phenomena.

_____

_____

_____

9. Conventional diets limit the amount of fat and increase the amount of carbohydrates, but high-protein diets are becoming popular, and many people are making bacon, steak, and butter part of their weight-loss plan.

_____

_____

_____

10. Lake Nicaragua was cut off from the Pacific Ocean by lava; it is ninety-six miles long and thirty-nine miles wide, and it is the only freshwater lake in the world to contain people-eating sharks.

_____

_____

_____

10.2 Subordination

- *Indicate which sentence in each of the following pairs is preferable because it uses proper subordination.*

EXAMPLE

_a_   a. In the Southwest one can visit prehistoric cliff dwellings, which were built into canyon walls.

       b. In the Southwest one can visit, which were built into canyon walls, prehistoric cliff dwellings.

_____ 1. a. Although Admiral Nelson was mortally wounded at the Battle of Trafalgar, he lived long enough to learn of the British victory.

       b. Admiral Nelson lived long enough to learn of the British victory, although he was mortally wounded in the Battle of Trafalgar.

_____ 2. a. Thomas Nast was a famous political cartoonist, and he originated the Republican elephant and the Democratic donkey, and he is also credited with creating the modern depiction of Santa Claus.

       b. Thomas Nast, the famous political cartoonist who originated the Republican elephant and the Democratic donkey, is also credited with creating the modern depiction of Santa Claus.

_____ 3. a. Identity theft, although this crime has existed for years, has become more common in recent times.

       b. Although identity theft has existed for years, this crime has become more common in recent times.

_____ 4. a. Winona traveled to Hawaii, when she stayed at a hotel near Diamond Head.

       b. Winona stayed at a hotel near Diamond Head when she traveled to Hawaii.

_____ 5. a. Affecting nearly 5 percent of America's children, learning disabilities are hard to overcome because they have multiple causes.

       b. Learning disabilities, which affect nearly 5 percent of America's children and have multiple causes, so they are hard to overcome.

_____ 6. a. Apple pie has been more popular since the end of the eighteenth century, although pumpkin pie was served a century earlier.

       b. Although pumpkin pie was served a century earlier, apple pie has been more popular since the end of the eighteenth century.

_____ 7. a. James Michener, who wrote the blockbuster novel *Hawaii* and who went on to win a Pulitzer Prize, penned over forty books and donated over $100 million to charities and schools.

b. Author of the blockbuster novel *Hawaii* and winner of the Pulitzer Prize, James Michener penned over forty books and donated over $100 million to charities and schools.

_____ 8. a. The CDC is a federal agency, and it has the responsibility to diagnose and trace the sources of infectious diseases, and it is located in Atlanta, Georgia.

b. The CDC, which is a federal agency responsible for diagnosing and tracing the sources of infectious diseases, is located in Atlanta, Georgia.

_____ 9. a. When he discovered several excellent restaurants in its French Quarter, Antonio visited New Orleans.

b. When Antonio visited New Orleans, he discovered several excellent restaurants in its French Quarter.

_____ 10. a. After intriguing generations of scientists, channel-like features on Mars have helped stimulate a search for water on the red planet.

b. Mars has channel-like features, and they have intrigued generations of scientists and more recently have helped stimulate a search for water on the red planet.

10.3 Subordination

- *Revise the following sentences to achieve effective subordination.*

EXAMPLE

Mosquitoes can transmit diseases, and many communities spray to kill them.

Because mosquitoes can transmit diseases, many communities spray to kill them.

1. Many television stations in the United States are on the air twenty-four hours a day, but in many foreign countries the number of broadcasting hours is regulated carefully.

    _____

    _____

    _____

    _____

2. Doctors urge pregnant women to eat well-balanced meals, and evidence shows that many adult diseases begin before birth.

    _____

    _____

    _____

    _____

3. The popularity of rap, reggae, and country music has increased steadily over the last ten years, and the sales of rock recordings have decreased.

    _____

    _____

    _____

    _____

4. Radio was a popular form of entertainment in the 1930s and 1940s, and many people thought television would be useful only for educational and public-information programs.

_____

_____

_____

_____

5. Clare Boothe Luce was the first woman to represent the United States in a major diplomatic post, and she also served two terms in Congress.

_____

_____

_____

_____

6. Sports utility vehicles continue to be popular, and they also provide comfort and a feeling of safety.

_____

_____

_____

_____

7. America witnessed an immigration boom in the 1990s, and it was almost as big as the immigration boom in the 1900s.

_____

_____

_____

_____

8. Orson Welles is best known for his production of a film, *Citizen Kane*, and he was twenty-six when he directed it.

_____

_____

_____

_____

9. Knute Rockne was a master strategist who coached the Notre Dame football team for thirteen years and whose team was undefeated in 1929 and 1930, his last two seasons.

_____

_____

_____

_____

10. The dean of students at a university is someone who often assists students who experience difficulties that are academic or personal.

_____

_____

_____

_____

10.4 Completeness and Comparisons

Make your sentences complete in structure and thought. Be careful when using *so, such,* and *too* in sentences, and do not omit necessary verbs and prepositions or the word *that*. Make your comparisons clear and complete by comparing only similar terms, using the word *other* where necessary, and avoiding awkward and incomplete comparisons.

■ *Revise the following sentences to correct any errors in completeness and comparisons.*

EXAMPLES
The old warehouse is too small.

The old warehouse is too small to hold the inventory.

Rafting on the Colorado River is more exciting than any river in the United States.

Rafting is more exciting on the Colorado River than on any other river in the United States.

1. The advertisement claimed that the new detergent was twice as strong.

_____

_____

2. Jeremy was so excited about his team's championship victory.

_____

_____

3. Carl Lewis has and continues to be called America's greatest track star, winning nine gold medals in the Olympics.

_____

_____

4. Chrysler says its new pickup truck is better.

_____

_____

5. Even casual viewers realize that Japanese kabuki theater is different.

_____

_____

6. Hiking across Nepal was better for her self-esteem.

_____

_____

7. She was both interested and concerned about living in a large foreign city.

_____

_____

8. The new investigative reporter was as good if not better than some of her more experienced coworkers.

_____

_____

9. Andrew Lloyd Webber's musical *Phantom of the Opera* is one of the most enjoyable if not popular in several years.

_____

_____

10. Maria likes quiche more than Sara.

_____

_____

10.5 Completeness and Comparisons

■ *Revise the following sentences to correct any errors in completeness and comparisons.*

EXAMPLE
No one works harder.

No one works harder than John. _____

1. Leasing a new car is sometimes more economical.

   _____

   _____

2. She bought a gerbil because she believed it would be a better house-hold pet.

   _____

   _____

3. Inexpensive, lightweight camcorders have already and will continue to be as influential as the telephone.

   _____

   _____

4. Installing a completely rebuilt engine is often cheaper.

   _____

   _____

5. Quilting is a more traditional hobby.

   _____

   _____

6. The lawyer was both involved and concerned about the trial's outcome.

_____

_____

7. For children, simple building blocks are as enjoyable if not more enjoyable than more expensive toys.

_____

_____

8. Paraguay is twice as large but only slightly more populous than Uruguay.

_____

_____

9. Jet skiing can be dangerous but it is more exciting.

_____

_____

10. Sri Lanka, formerly Ceylon, has and continues to be the world's chief supplier of natural cinnamon.

_____

_____

10.6 Consistency

■ *Revise the following sentences to make them structurally consistent. Avoid unnecessary shifts in tense, person, mood, or voice and shifts from one type of pronoun to another.*

EXAMPLES
Visibility was restricted to fifty feet when the airplane tries to take off.

Visibility was restricted to fifty feet when the airplane tried to take off.

[revised for consistency in tense]

When I traveled to the mountains of the Northwest, you can see great varieties of plant life.

When I traveled to the mountains of the Northwest, I saw great varieties of plant life.

[revised for consistency in person and tense]

1. To this day, most tourists were amazed by the ancient ruins of Petra, which contain many temples carved directly into sheer sandstone bluffs.

   _____

   _____

2. When the shooting started, he runs for cover.

   _____

   _____

3. We thought a light at the end of the tunnel is a sign of hope, but it was just on a train coming in our direction.

   _____

   _____

4. Dreams are not necessarily accidental, for they often were considered efforts of the subconscious to work out real problems.

_____

_____

5. After he buys an iguana, he realized how difficult it is to raise.

_____

_____

6. The cheetah is very tired after chasing its quarry and usually rested for several minutes before it ate.

_____

_____

7. The woman discovered the real identity of her friend after she knows her for twenty years.

_____

_____

8. Anyone planning to hike the Appalachian Trail needs to anticipate all the hazards they might encounter.

_____

_____

9. One should always remember to check your parachute before exiting an airplane.

_____

_____

10. First, an application form needs to be filled out by job candidates. Then she should ask for an interview.

_____

_____

10.7 Sentence Structure: Review 1

■ *Revise the following paragraph, correcting all shifts in person and excessive subordination.*

Mankind has long dreamed of traveling to Mars, and for the first time in history, interplanetary journey seems possible. What motives can propel humanity into the cold expanse of space, even to our closest planetary neighbor? Some reasons commonly given are merely silly. Traveling to Mars in order to establish a future home for humans, as some have suggested, makes no sense. The red planet's harsh temperatures, thin atmosphere, and scarcity of water make it no substitute for Earth's green, temperate surface. Other reasons are more compelling. By comparing Mars and Earth, you can better understand the history—and perhaps the future—of our planet. Furthermore, a mission piloted by humans to our closest planetary neighbor could answer, once and for all, the question "Does extraterrestrial life exist?" If discovered, such life would radically alter how you understand our place in the universe. Finally, the peaceful, transnational cooperation that such an enterprise would demand could only enhance life in *this* world, at least for the nations involved.

10.8 Sentence Structure: Review 2

■ *Revise the following paragraph, supplying any missing words and correcting all shifts in person, mood, and tense.*

The custom of the birthday cake began the thirteenth century in Germany, part of a day-long celebration called *Kinderfest*—or "child festival"—marking the birthday of a child. *Kinderfest* begins at dawn when you were awakened by the arrival of a cake topped with lighted candles. The one candle more than the total of the child's years represented the "light of life." The candles are burned and replaced all day until the cake is eaten after dinner. At this time you made a wish and blew out the candles. The candles had to be extinguished a single breath. For the wish to come true, it has to remain a secret.

Adapted from Charles Panati, *Extraordinary Origins of Everyday Things*
(New York: Harper, 1987), 33.

11 Position of Modifiers, Separation of Elements, Parallelism, and Sentence Variety

MODIFIERS

A modifier is a word or a group of words that limits or describes another word. Attach modifiers to the correct word or element in the sentence to avoid confusion. Most adjectives precede the nouns they modify. Adverbs may come before or follow the words they modify. Prepositional phrases usually follow the words they modify, as do adjective clauses. Adverbial phrases and clauses can be placed in various positions.

EXAMPLES

The *new* forms are finished. [adjective before the noun]

The auditions *soon* ended. [adverb before the verb]

The auditions ended *soon.* [adverb after the verb]

The aquarium *by the window* contains only guppies. [prepositional phrase modifying *aquarium*]

The lady came *to the door.* [prepositional phrase modifying *came*]

Sooner than we expected, the movie ended. [adverbial clause modifying *ended*]

The movie ended *sooner than we expected.* [adverbial clause modifying *ended*]

DANGLING MODIFIERS

A dangling modifier is a modifier that is not clearly attached to a word or element in a sentence. Avoid dangling modifiers. A verbal phrase at the beginning of a sentence should logically modify the subject.

Dangling Participle

UNCLEAR

Seeing the whales surface nearby, my excitement grew.

CLEAR

Seeing the whales surface nearby, I became excited.

Dangling Infinitive

UNCLEAR

To get an early start, *the alarm clock* was set for 6 A.M.

CLEAR

To get an early start, *I set* the alarm clock for 6 A.M.

Dangling Prepositional Phrase

UNCLEAR

While *in school,* my mother did her shopping.

CORRECT

While *I was* in school, my mother did her shopping.

MISPLACED AND SQUINTING MODIFIERS

Almost any modifier that comes between an adjective clause and the word it modifies can cause confusion.

UNCLEAR

Many people are questioned by grand juries *who may be innocent.*

CLEAR

Many people *who may be innocent* are questioned by grand juries.

A modifier placed between two words so that it can modify either word is a **squinting modifier.**

UNCLEAR

The chess master who was playing *calmly* won the first game.

CLEAR

The chess master who was *calmly* playing won the first game.

SEPARATION OF ELEMENTS

Do not separate closely related elements, such as the subject and the verb, parts of a verb phrase, or a verb and an object.

AWKWARD

The construction workers *had,* for a week, *expected* a new contract.

IMPROVED

For a week, the construction workers *had expected* a new contract.

Avoid **split infinitives** (modifiers between *to* and the verb form).

NOT

to actively *pursue*

BUT

to pursue actively

PARALLELISM

Make constructions in a sentence parallel (balanced) by matching phrase with phrase, clause with clause, verb with verb, and so on.

FAULTY

The men argued *bitterly* and *were loud.*

IMPROVED

The men argued *bitterly* and *loudly.*

Repeat an article (*a, an,* or *the*), a preposition (*by, in, for,* and so on), or other words to preserve parallelism and clarity.

FAULTY

The aircraft was *in a storm* and *trouble.*

IMPROVED

The aircraft was *in a storm* and *in trouble.*

SENTENCE VARIETY

Vary sentences in structure and order. Use loose, periodic, balanced, and inverted sentence forms.

- A **loose sentence** makes its main point at the beginning of the sentence and then adds qualifications or refinements.

  We left early, missing the heavy traffic.

- A **periodic sentence** saves the main point until the end of a sentence to create suspense or emphasis.

  After a long afternoon visiting my aunt, I was exhausted.

- A **balanced sentence** has parallel parts in terms of structure, length, and thoughts.

  We must work so that we may live, not live so that we may work.

- An **inverted sentence** reverses the usual subject-verb-object or subject-verb-complement order of declarative sentences.

  Incalculable are the thoughts of infants.

11.1 Position of Modifiers

■ *Revise the following sentences to correct faulty modifiers.*

EXAMPLE
Some of the reporters were insistent who questioned the candidate.

Some of the reporters who questioned the candidate were

insistent.

1. The waitress brought our entrées with a friendly smile.

    _____

    _____

2. Some animal trainers consider dogs strongly to be the most domesti-
   cated animal.

    _____

    _____

3. Mountaineers successfully scale tall peaks who are well prepared.

    _____

    _____

4. In 1819, the United States bought Florida wisely from Spain for five million dollars.

    _____

    _____

5. The new stadium will cost less fortunately than the original estimate.

    _____

    _____

6. Suddenly reaching an arm through the bars of the cage, the man's pocket was torn by the monkey.

_____

_____

7. Running poorly and rusting quickly, I decided to repair my old car.

_____

_____

8. Before submitting the project for a grade, the instructor insisted that we check our work carefully.

_____

_____

9. Hikers waded the stream climbing to the summit.

_____

_____

10. They decided with real estate prices dropping quickly to sell their house.

_____

_____

158

11.2 Position of Modifiers

■ *Revise the following sentences to correct faulty modifiers.*

EXAMPLE
The air traffic controller who worked cautiously brought in Flight 89.

Working cautiously, the air traffic controller brought in Flight 89.

[corrected for a squinting modifier]

1. Blue lights pulsing, I saw the police car speed through the intersection and disappear around the corner.

   _____

   _____

2. Before being tested, the engineer brought the experimental equipment to the laboratory.

   _____

   _____

3. Hoping to see a polar bear, every fall thousands of tourists visit Churchill, Manitoba.

   _____

   _____

4. The exhausted runner looked eagerly for the finish line, nearing the end of his first marathon.

   _____

   _____

5. Wondering what to do next, the clock struck midnight.

   _____

   _____

6. Receiving a substantial raise, the worker's house could be repaired.

_____

_____

7. Unlike black bears, campers must remember that grizzlies can be very aggressive.

_____

_____

8. Getting married often brings out the best in people.

_____

_____

9. To play golf well, daily practice is necessary.

_____

_____

10. Many candidates promise openly to deal with controversial issues.

_____

_____

11.3 Separation of Elements

Do not separate closely related elements unnecessarily. Separation of parts of a verb phrase, a verb and its object, or a subject and its verb can be awkward or misleading.

■ *Revise the following sentences by correcting unnecessarily separated elements.*

EXAMPLE
Yellowstone Park, for many years, has been known as the site of Old Faithful.

For many years, Yellowstone Park has been known as the site of
Old Faithful.

1. The Munchkins, during the filming of *The Wizard of Oz,* made $50 a week and worked twelve hours a day, six days a week.

   _____

   _____

2. Irving Berlin wrote, to the surprise of many, "God Bless America" twenty years before Kate Smith introduced it in 1938.

   _____

   _____

3. After the debris was, by the Army Corps of Engineers, cleared, the stream dropped below flood stage.

   _____

   _____

4. Darwin did not expect his book *On the Origin of Species* to as profoundly affect the scientific world as it did.

   _____

   _____

5. Linotype machines, invented by Ottmar Mergenthaler and first used by the *New York Tribune* in 1886, cast a full line of type at a time.

_____

_____

6. The coal reserves of the United States for three hundred years can meet current energy demands.

_____

_____

7. Many people, despite high interest rates, make only the minimum required payments on their credit card balances each month.

_____

_____

8. Women biologists, by examining how females affect the behavior of various species, have changed our understanding of nature.

_____

_____

9. The saxophonist who learned the drill most quickly was elected section leader.

_____

_____

10. Dominique believed, although none of her teammates did, that she would win an athletic scholarship.

_____

_____

11.4 Parallelism

Parallelism means that corresponding parts of a sentence are similar in structure, length, and thought.

■ *Revise the following sentences to correct faulty parallelism.*

EXAMPLE
Computerized inventory control can save time, ensure adequate stock, and is helpful in keeping track of sales trends.

Computerized inventory control can save time, ensure adequate stock, and help keep track of sales trends.

1. Americans invented jazz as well as developing rock and roll.

   _____

   _____

2. Dragonflies can fly twenty-five miles per hour, take off backwards, and they have a 360-degree field of vision.

   _____

   _____

3. Alarmed by the hunters' guns, the ducks rose quickly from the water and were noisy as they flew to safety.

   _____

   _____

4. Guests at the inn enjoyed fine dining, great scenery, and the weather was very beautiful.

   _____

   _____

5. Annoyed at the long checkout lines, the shopper began to sigh loudly, tapping his foot, and glance at his watch.

_____

_____

6. The mail carrier opened the gate, walked to the door, and then he put the letters in the mailbox.

_____

_____

7. The physician advised her patient to eat sensibly, drink moderately, and exercise.

_____

_____

8. At school she found that she enjoyed living in the dormitory, new friends, and economics.

_____

_____

9. Several proven ways to relieve stress include massage, meditation, and exercising regularly.

_____

_____

10. The sun was hot, but the breeze was cool, the seas were calm, and there were crowds of people on the beach.

_____

_____

11.5 Parallelism

■ *Revise the following sentences to correct faulty parallelism.*

EXAMPLE
The new decor is in good taste and attractive.

The new decor is tasteful and attractive. _____

1. Indoor theme parks use computers, sit-in simulators as well as watching movies through 3-D glasses to replicate the thrills of traditional theme parks.

   _____

   _____

2. The superstitious English of the sixteenth and seventeenth centuries were afraid of moonless nights, and black cats terrified them.

   _____

   _____

3. When the play finished its run on Broadway, the lead actor said he was tired but that he was pleased with his performance.

   _____

   _____

4. The museum either needs some new exhibits or some better tour guides.

   _____

   _____

5. The Egyptians introduced stone architecture and also are credited with developing the 365-day calendar.

   _____

   _____

6. Good economists not only measure the confidence of consumers but also what percentage of the work force is employed.

_____

_____

7. His parents will feel successful if he graduates, finds a decent job, and if he can stay out of trouble.

_____

_____

8. The assembly line was not only physically exhausting, but it was easy to get confused.

_____

_____

9. The coach divided his players into groups based on size, how fast they were, and the number of years they had played.

_____

_____

10. Microwave foods have become very popular because of ease of preparation, they cook quickly, and often are delicious.

_____

_____

11.6 Variety in Sentences

A **loose sentence** makes its main point at the beginning of the sentence and then adds qualifications or refinements. A **periodic sentence** saves the main point until the end of the sentence to create suspense or emphasis. A **balanced sentence** has parallel parts in terms of structure, length, and thoughts.

■ *Identify the following sentences as loose or periodic.*

EXAMPLES

When wind speeds exceed seventy-five miles an hour, a tropical storm is called a hurricane.

_____*periodic*_____

A tropical storm is called a hurricane when its wind speeds exceed seventy-five miles an hour.

_____*loose*_____

1. After the moon had risen over the forest, the mouth of the underground passageway leading to the ancient shrine became dimly visible.

_____

2. Black Friday usually refers to September 19, 1873, when numerous business failures inaugurated the panic of 1873.

_____

3. After the refinisher stripped the varnish from the chair, she sanded it thoroughly.

_____

4. Ecotourism allows well-heeled travelers a glimpse of unspoiled nature; archaeological tours offer them unique insight into the past.

_____

5. Before William Faulkner became a famous novelist, he worked in a Mississippi post office.

_____

6. A large crowd quickly gathered on the shore when vacationers heard reports of a beached whale.

_____

7. On the last day of their visit to Washington, the group spent an hour at the Vietnam Memorial.

_____

8. If the ancient Greeks can be called the great philosophers of the classical world, the ancient Romans can be called its great engineers.

_____

9. Even though grits are now a staple of Southern cuisine, the dish did not become common until after the Civil War. _____

10. Although most states have laws and regulations that control interest rates, in many instances the laws are either confusing or contradictory. _____

11.7 Variety in Sentences

■ *Make the following loose sentences into periodic ones.*

EXAMPLE
The liver is an irreplaceable organ of the body, for machines cannot duplicate its various and highly complex functions.

Machines cannot duplicate the various and highly complex bodily
functions of one irreplaceable organ of the body, the liver.

1. Ancient Rome was the first society governed by a bicameral legislature.

_____

_____

2. Charles Dickens's *A Christmas Carol* quickly sold over six thousand copies, largely because of its author's popularity.

_____

_____

3. One must cross the bridge at Oregon Inlet to reach Hatteras Island by road.

_____

_____

4. Today many cartoons are designed for adult viewers, although some people still associate animation with children.

_____

_____

5. Neil Armstrong was the first person to set foot on the moon.

_____

_____

6. South Dakota is nicknamed the Sunshine State, though many people prefer to call it the Coyote State.

_____

_____

7. Southeastern Oregon is largely unpopulated because it is a harsh, alkaline desert.

_____

_____

8. Geographic regions of the United States may experience severe financial stress before the nation as a whole meets the established criteria for a recession.

_____

_____

9. Every stamp collector wants a 1928 Graf Zeppelin stamp because it is very rare.

_____

_____

10. You need to get written estimates from several suppliers if you want the best possible price.

_____

_____

11.8 Variety in Sentences

A **loose sentence** makes the main point early and then adds refinements. A **periodic sentence** withholds an element of the main thought until the end and thus creates suspense and emphasis. A **balanced sentence** has parts that are similar in structure and length and that express parallel thoughts.

■ *Make one sentence out of each of the groups below. Vary your sentences in length, structure, and order. Write simple, compound, and complex patterns, and use loose, periodic, and balanced forms.*

EXAMPLE
The Liberty Bell was rung only twice.
It now sits in Independence Hall.
Independence Hall is in Philadelphia.

The Liberty Bell, which now sits in Independence Hall, Philadelphia, was rung only twice.

1. The rain forests of Malaysia cover half the nation.
   They contain as many as one thousand different species of plants per acre.
   They are protected by many laws.

   _____

   _____

   _____

   _____

2. Mount Everest was named in 1855.
   It was named for Sir George Everest.
   He was a surveyor general of India.

   _____

   _____

   _____

   _____

3. George Pullman built the first dining car in 1868.
   The car was named *Delmonico*.
   The name of the car came from a famous family of New York City restaurateurs.

   _____

   _____

   _____

   _____

4. The Indian kingdom of Quito was in the area that is now called Ecuador.
   It was over two thousand years old when the Incas conquered it.
   They conquered it in 1487.

   _____

   _____

   _____

   _____

5. Clothing made of synthetic materials has been popular since World War II.
   Cotton is becoming popular again.
   Cotton fabric is well suited for summer sportswear.

   _____

   _____

   _____

   _____

6. The Red Sea is one of the world's busiest waterways.
   It has some of the saltiest water in the world.
   It has many coral reefs.

   _____

   _____

_____

_____

7. For more than one hundred years, visitors to Atlantic City, New Jersey,
   have admired the work of professional sand sculptors.
   These sculptors first worked directly in the sand.
   Later, they worked on wooden frames.

_____

_____

_____

_____

8. Arthur Rackham was an English artist.
   He illustrated many children's books, including *Mother Goose, Alice's
   Adventures in Wonderland,* and *Rip Van Winkle.*
   His work is distinguished by its rich, imaginative detail.

_____

_____

_____

_____

9. Soft contact lenses are quite popular.
   They require more care than hard contact lenses do.
   Soft lenses must be washed daily and cleaned with a special solution
   once a month.

_____

_____

_____

_____

10. Columbus is supposed to have discovered America in the fifteenth century.

Norsemen are credited with discovering the New World about A.D. 1000.

The first people to find the New World probably crossed a land bridge connecting Siberia and Alaska between 18,000 and 14,000 B.C.

_____

_____

_____

_____

NAME _____

DATE _____ SCORE _____

11.9 Sentence Structure: Review 1

■ *Rewrite the following paragraph to eliminate nonparallel structures as well as dangling and misplaced modifiers.*

The word *Yankee* has an interesting history, but it is of uncertain origin. Some people believe the word came from Europe, where natives of the Netherlands were sometimes called *Jan Kees;* it is the opinion of others that the word is derived from *anglais,* the French word for English, or perhaps from a Native American pronunciation of the word *English.* Made popular during the Revolutionary War, people of other countries now use the word *Yankee* to refer to any American. Most Americans, though, use the word to refer to New Englanders, while in the states that once belonged to the Confederacy, *Yankee* is used as a term of opprobrium still to refer to anyone who lives in what were the Union states during the American Civil War.

11.10 Sentence Structure: Review 2

- *Combine the following kernel sentences into an effective paragraph. Make equivalent sentences parallel and use balanced, loose, and periodic sentences to provide appropriate emphasis.*

1. The Cherokees have lived in the southern Appalachian Mountains for over two thousand years.
2. Linguists believe they are related to the Iroquois of New York.

3. In 1540, they met Europeans for the first time.
4. At that time they controlled a large area.
5. The area was three times the size of Virginia.
6. It stretched from the Ohio River to the Chattahoochee.

7. Their civilization was advanced.
8. They lived in sixty villages.
9. They planted corn, tobacco, and beans.
10. They numbered about 25,000.

11. By 1830, they had a constitutional government.
12. The government included a senate.
13. It included a house of representatives.
14. It included a chief who was elected.
15. They had a written language.
16. They had a newspaper.
17. They had schools.

18. In 1830, Andrew Jackson signed the Indian Removal Act.
19. This act said that no Native American tribes could live east of the Mississippi River.

20. The Cherokees appealed to the United States Supreme Court.
21. Chief Justice John Marshall ruled that they had the right to live in Georgia.
22. They were rounded up anyway.

23. Between 1838 and 1839, fifteen thousand were deported to Oklahoma.
24. About a thousand hid in the Great Smoky Mountains.
25. Their descendants live in the area to this day.

Adapted from Geoffrey Norman, "The Cherokee,"
National Geographic 187, no. 5 (1999): 72–97.

Punctuation

12 Commas

USES OF COMMAS

Although commas have many functions, they are used, in general, to separate elements and to set off modifiers or parenthetical elements.

Between Two Independent Clauses

Use the comma to separate independent clauses joined by a coordinating conjunction (*and, but, or, nor, for, so, yet*).

> The brisk winds raised only moderate waves, *but* the falling barometer indicated that stormy weather was coming.

In a Series

Use a comma between words, phrases, and clauses in a series of three or more.

> Politicians often address business groups, civic organizations, and school assemblies. [phrases in a series]

> The audience was seated, the overture had begun, and the curtain was about to go up. [clauses in a series]

Between Coordinate Adjectives

Use a comma between coordinate adjectives not joined by *and*. Coordinate adjectives each modify the noun (or pronoun) independently.

> The *gloomy, uninhabited* house was very isolated.

Cumulative adjectives do not modify independently. Do not use a comma between cumulative adjectives.

> He discarded his *favorite blue* sweater.

NOTE: To recognize coordinate adjectives, place the word *and* between them and determine whether they sound right.

> The gloomy *and* uninhabited house was isolated. [sounds right]

> He discarded his favorite *and* blue sweater. [sounds wrong]

Another test is to reverse the adjectives. Normally, coordinate adjectives are easily reversible.

uninhabited, gloomy house [sounds right]

blue favorite sweater [sounds wrong]

After Long Introductory Clauses or Phrases

Use a comma after a long introductory phrase or clause.

Shortly after the abrupt end of the first act, everyone was certain that the butler had committed the crime. [phrase]

When the first act came to an abrupt end, everyone was certain that the butler had committed the crime. [clause]

An introductory verbal phrase is usually set off by a comma.

Working alone, she built a new room at the mountain retreat. [participial phrase]

To prepare for the race, the runner trained for weeks. [infinitive phrase]

With Nonrestrictive Elements

Use commas to set off nonrestrictive appositives, phrases, and clauses that add description or information but are not essential to the meaning of the sentence.

Geri, the Northside branch manager, expects to be transferred soon. [nonrestrictive appositive phrase]

Geri, who is the Northside branch manager, expects to be transferred soon. [nonrestrictive adjective clause]

Mount Saint Helens, dormant for a long period, erupted with great fury. [nonrestrictive adjective phrase]

Note that a restrictive element is necessary for the meaning of the total sentence and that it is not set off by commas.

The music *that we most enjoy* is contemporary.

With Conjunctive Adverbs

Use a comma after a conjunctive adverb (*however, nevertheless, moreover, furthermore,* and so on) when it precedes an independent clause.

The profit margin was down; *however,* next year should be better.

With Sentence Elements Out of Normal Word Order

Use commas with sentence elements out of normal word order.

The trainer, *haggard and thin,* slowly saddled the horse.

With Degrees, Titles, Dates, Places, Addresses

Use commas with degrees and titles as well as to separate elements in dates, places, and addresses.

Rosa Adams, M.D., joined the staff. [comma before and after *M.D.*]

On March 10, 1971, my daughter was born. [comma before and after year]

On Monday, December 19, the Christmas vacation begins. [comma before and after date]

Sedona, Arizona, is at the entrance to Oak Creek Canyon. [Use a comma before and after the name of a state when the city is named.]

BUT

In July 1969 we bought a new home. [optional commas]

The year 1945 marked the end of World War II. [no comma]

My new address is 196 Warner Avenue, Westwood, CA 73520. [no comma before zip code]

For Contrast or Emphasis

Use commas for contrast and emphasis as well as for short interrogative elements.

Many doctors believe that exercise, not diet, is the key to weight loss.

The sheep continued eating, not sensing the cougar's presence.

You have read this before, haven't you?

With Mild Interjections and *Yes* or *No*

Use commas with mild interjections and with words like *yes* and *no*.

Well, I was almost right.

Yes, we agree to your offer.

With Direct Address

Use commas with words in direct address.

"Laura, did you receive this letter?"

Use commas with expressions like *he said* or *she replied* when used with quoted matter.

"I cannot find my raincoat," *he complained.*

With Absolute Phrases

Set off an absolute phrase with a comma. An absolute phrase, which consists of a noun followed by a modifier, modifies an entire sentence.

The restaurant being closed, we decided to go home.

To Prevent Misreading or to Mark an Omission

Use commas to prevent misreading or to mark an omission.

Above, the wind howled through the trees.

The summer days were hot and dry; the nights, warm and humid. [comma for omitted verb *were*]

12.1 Commas with Independent Clauses

■ *In the following sentences, insert and circle commas between independent clauses. In the blank at right, enter the comma and the coordinating conjunction. If a sentence is correct, write* **C.**

EXAMPLE

The wheel of fortune was a significant symbol in many ancient cultures, and it appears in the works of both Dante and Chaucer.

_____*, and*_____

1. About one-third of the passengers on the *Mayflower* left England for religious reasons and the other two-thirds were adventurers.

_____

2. Rottweilers were bred in Germany but they are descended from dogs that invading Roman armies used to herd cattle.

_____

3. The winter was unusually warm so Alison and her friends had to postpone their skiing trip.

_____

4. The numerals we use today are commonly known as Arabic numerals but were actually invented by the people of India and are sometimes called Hindu numerals.

_____

5. The Vedas are the oldest Hindu scriptures and some were composed as early as 1000 B.C.

_____

6. The value of a beach rental property depends upon its size, its popularity, and its condition.

_____

7. More than twenty-seven million acres of Alaska belong to national forests, parks, and monuments and the best-known park is probably Denali National Park. _____

8. Many patients now receive organ transplants but doctors still do not know how many years these transplants will continue to function. _____

9. Jeannette Rankin was the first woman elected to the U.S. Congress and the only member of the House to vote against entering World War II. _____

10. Three invertebrate animals have become extinct in the last three hundred years and this is well above nature's normal rate of extinction. _____

12.2 Commas with Independent Clauses

■ *In the following sentences, insert and circle commas between independent clauses. In the blank at the right, enter the comma and the coordinating conjunction. If a sentence is correct, write* **C.**

EXAMPLE

Polls are not always reliable, but most companies still use them.   _____, but_____

The use of alcohol as automotive fuel is hardly a new idea, for Henry Ford designed the Model T to use it.   _____, for_____

1. Babe Ruth pitched twenty-nine scoreless innings in the 1916 and 1918 World Series but he is best known for his long-standing home run record.   _____

2. The first true cameras were not invented until the 1820s so we rely upon paintings and sculpture to see the likenesses of great and ordinary people from the past.   _____

3. Many students seek part-time employment during their vacations so unemployment rates rise during the summer months.   _____

4. Lady Astor was the wife of Waldorf Astor and the first woman member of the British House of Commons.   _____

5. Regional networks for sports soon will become standard fare on cable television but for the time being nationwide sporting events dominate.   _____

6. Self-employed farmers contribute to Social Security at the same rate as other self-employed people for farmers are considered to be independent small-business people. _____

7. The small painting being auctioned was by a relatively minor sixteenth-century artist but it was valued at almost a quarter of a million dollars. _____

8. DVD technology is rapidly changing the way we watch movies at home and will replace magnetic tapes in the near future. _____

9. Weekend athletes exert themselves only sporadically yet they are surprised when they suffer minor sprains and other injuries. _____

10. Ultrasound technology can help determine the age of a fetus and identify certain birth defects. _____

12.3 Commas with Items in a Series

Use a comma between words, phrases, and clauses in a series of three or more.

■ *Insert and circle commas as necessary in items in a series.*

EXAMPLE

Charities solicit funds from businesses, civic groups, and individuals.

1. The Pleiades Taurus and Orion are three of the best-known winter constellations in the Northern Hemisphere.

2. American English continually drops old words adds new ones and develops new connotations for familiar expressions.

3. In the 1800s, phrenologists believed they could identify such character traits as caution kindness and conscientiousness by examining the shape of a person's skull.

4. Office desks often come equipped with space for computers modems and fax machines.

5. The swimmers were expected to win the freestyle backstroke and butterfly events.

6. Before studying, Elaine always sharpens three pencils straightens her desk and fills her notebook with paper.

7. "We have sealed all the hatches taken in all the sails and radioed for help," wrote the desperate sea captain.

8. Kenya took the gold medal Morocco the silver and Germany the bronze.

9. Many pioneers began their journey west carrying little more than a rifle an ax a plowshare and a few simple carpentry tools.

10. A number of political parties, including the Federalist Party the Whig Party and the Democratic-Republican Party, played important roles in America's past.

12.4 Commas with Coordinate Adjectives

Use a comma between coordinate adjectives not joined by *and*. Coordinate adjectives each modify the noun (or pronoun) independently.

■ *Insert and circle commas as necessary between coordinate adjectives.*

EXAMPLE

The garden court is a new, exciting concept in motel design.

1. Radio talk shows attract many outspoken opinionated callers.

2. Two of the world's largest arid regions, the Sahara Desert and the Kalahari Desert, lie in Africa.

3. The small hardy Lapps speak a language related to Finnish.

4. Many corporations are looking for employees with sound liberal arts backgrounds as well as aggressive entrepreneurial personalities.

5. The artist took a slow careful look at her finished canvas.

6. The rock star tossed his long curly hair at the camera during the interview.

7. Modern farmers use systemic cotton defoliants to allow mechanical harvesters easier access to opened bolls.

8. Builders use strong lightweight plywood in almost every kind of construction.

9. More Americans are becoming familiar with the sharp piercing cry of the coyote.

10. "Laughter, I believe, is the best least expensive medicine," said the speaker.

12.5 Commas After Introductory Clauses or Phrases

■ *Place and circle commas as needed after introductory clauses or phrases. In the blank at the right, place the comma and write the word after it. If a sentence is punctuated correctly or requires no punctuation, write* **C.**

EXAMPLE
When mortgage rates are high, realtors seek alternatives to conventional financing.

, realtors

1. Built in 1769 and used to pull French artillery the world's first automobile, a steam carriage, was invented by Captain Nicolas Cugnot.

_____

2. As the first American college to confer degrees on women Oberlin College traditionally has been a leader in higher education.

_____

3. After discovering the relation between bacteria and infection Joseph Lister revolutionized medicine by developing antiseptic surgical procedures.

_____

4. Because oil paint dries slowly and does not crack artists have favored it for hundreds of years.

_____

5. If no one claims the estate by next week everything will be sold at auction.

_____

6. Its leafy shade harboring many forms of life the old oak towered over the surrounding fields and pastureland.

_____

7. Covering more than 650,000 square miles the Great Artesian Basin is an important underground source of water in eastern Australia. _____

8. To strengthen her back and legs the high jumper began a rigorous weight-lifting program. _____

9. Although the destruction of ancient Pompeii was tragic its ruins have allowed modern archaeologists an unusually detailed view of Roman life. _____

10. The rookie driver would have won his first race easily if he had not run out of fuel during the last lap. _____

12.6 Commas After Introductory Clauses or Phrases

■ *Place and circle commas as needed after introductory clauses or phrases. In the blank at the right, place the comma and write the word after it. If a sentence is punctuated correctly or requires no punctuation, write* **C.**

EXAMPLE

Although most engineers are college graduates, they may need continual technical training.

_____ *, they* _____

1. Soon after the laser was created in 1960 scientists began searching for ways to use it in medicine. _____

2. Although the word *hound* once referred to any kind of dog it now chiefly refers to certain types of hunting dogs. _____

3. Even though computers today have reached an amazing level of speed and sophistication future computer chips may perform 250 million calculations each second. _____

4. Almost twice the size of the United States Siberia contains only one-sixth as many people. _____

5. Mounting his war steed with the help of a ladder Pippin the Short marshaled his troops for battle. _____

6. In 1859 Edwin C. Drake drilled the nation's first oil well and inaugurated the modern oil industry. _____

7. During her tours of duty with NATO forces in Europe Captain Nichols learned to speak both German and French. _____

8. Because they are affectionate and can learn to talk, parrots are a favorite pet among bird lovers. _____

9. Completed in 432 B.C. the Parthenon is the best surviving example of classical Greek architecture. _____

10. To get the best deals some people will show up at yard sales two hours early. _____

12.7 Commas with Nonrestrictive Elements

Use commas to set off nonrestrictive appositives, phrases, and clauses that add description or information but are *not* essential to the meaning of the sentence.

■ *Correctly punctuate nonrestrictive elements in the following sentences. Circle punctuation that you add. Write* **C** *to the right of any correctly punctuated sentence.*

EXAMPLE

Janice, who is our first choice for the position, has accepted a job with another company.

1. Nylon which can be woven into delicate lingerie can also be fashioned into durable machinery parts.

2. Optometrists who are allowed to prescribe glasses are not allowed to use surgery or drugs to treat their patients.

3. Air bags which were once considered impractical luxury items are now standard equipment on many vehicles.

4. The pine-tree shilling was one of several coins that were minted in the American colonies before the Revolutionary War.

5. The potato is one of the major food crops that originated in the Americas.

6. We couldn't tell which signatures were forged or which were genuine.

7. Bald eagles which can be found mainly in wilderness areas usually prefer a diet of fish.

8. Aaron rewarded the boy who found and returned his wallet.

9. Professional counseling in elementary school which is a relatively new field can make a dramatic difference in the scholastic performance of young children.

197

10. John Donne who was born into a Catholic family was the dean of St. Paul's Cathedral and the most famous Anglican sermon writer of his day.

12.8 Commas—All Uses

■ *Correctly punctuate the following sentences. Circle punctuation that you add.*

EXAMPLE
Denver, Colorado, and San Diego, California, are two of the most rapidly growing cities in the United States.

1. The meeting scheduled for Tuesday January 15 has been postponed until Thursday January 24.

2. Wendel Patterson Ph.D. joined the international think tank of Blackwood Mauldon and Banks on June 30 1954.

3. Sequoia National Park established on September 25 1890 is the nation's second-oldest national park.

4. Often called the Prairie Provinces Alberta Saskatchewan and Manitoba produce most of Canada's cattle and grain.

5. To understand the British system of nobility which is usually referred to as the peerage one needs to know something of British history.

6. Shakespeare's sonnets 154 in all were first published in 1609 though Shakespeare had circulated them in manuscript form among his friends before that date.

7. The American Council of Learned Societies which sponsors many kinds of fellowships in various academic disciplines is located at 345 East 46th Street New York NY 10017.

8. Its back wheels spinning helplessly the sports car slid off the icy road and into the ditch.

9. The Spanish explorers who followed Columbus to the Caribbean discovered small amounts of gold as well as fierce resistance by the Caribs, a warlike tribe.

10. Ruth Bader Ginsberg the second woman to be appointed to the U.S. Supreme Court began serving in 1994.

12.9 Commas: Review 1

■ *Revise the following paragraph to correct all errors in the use of commas.*

Well-known since Charles Darwin made them his laboratory in the 1830s the Galapagos Islands are famous for their giant tortoises and marine iguanas. Located some six hundred miles off the coast of Ecuador these islands still have secrets to unveil. Many of these are underwater however and explorers are just beginning to discover them. Darwin and his contemporaries only caught a glimpse of the undersea world through glass-bottomed buckets. Early in the next century divers donned scuba gear and descended as far as two hundred feet. At the end of that century intrepid divers used a small submersible to descend more than 1500 feet. The cold dark world they entered was teeming with life including squid sea cucumbers sharks goosefish and transparent eels. A series of dives yielded a dozen new species of vertebrate animals. A laboratory for Darwin the Galapagos it seems still have much to reveal.

Adapted from John F. Ross, "IMAX Takes Us Undersea in the Galapagos,"
Smithsonian 30, no. 7 (1999): 52–64.

12.10 Commas: Review 2

■ *Revise the following paragraph to correct all errors in the use of commas.*

Samuel Johnson one of England's most colorful men of letters lived a life filled with contradictions. He was a scholarly man fluent in Greek Latin and French but he welcomed many poor uneducated people into his household. Although a deeply religious man he frequently suffered from religious doubts. He had a reputation for sloth yet he almost single-handedly compiled the first comprehensive English dictionary a remarkable feat when one considers that he was nearly blind as a result of a childhood case of scrofula. Although his contemporaries knew him as a poet an essayist and a brilliant conversation-alist he is perhaps best remembered today as a lexicographer.

13   Unnecessary Commas

Do not use commas excessively. Placing commas at all pauses in sentences is not a correct practice.

Between Subject and Verb

Do not use a comma between subject and verb, between verb or verbal and complement, or between an adjective and the word it modifies.

INCORRECT

The team with the best record, will go to the playoffs. [Delete comma.]

We saw, that the window had been left open. [Delete comma.]

The shining wrapping, paper caught one's attention. [Delete comma.]

Between Compound Elements

Do not use a comma between compound elements such as verbs, subjects, complements, and predicates.

INCORRECT

We went to the local library, and perused the *New York Times.* [Delete comma.]

Between Dependent Clauses

Do not use a comma before a coordinating conjunction joining two dependent clauses.

INCORRECT

We checked to see that the lights were off, and that all the doors were locked. [Delete comma.]

In Comparisons

Do not use a comma before *than* in a comparison or between compound conjunctions such as *as . . . as, so . . . so, so . . . that.*

INCORRECT

The electrician found more wrong with the washing machine, than we had expected. [Delete comma.]

It was so hot, that the engine overheated. [Delete comma.]

After *Like* or *Such As*

Do not use a comma after *like* or *such as*. A comma is used before *such as* only when the phrase is nonrestrictive.

INCORRECT

Many famous paintings such as, the *Mona Lisa* and *View of Toledo* are almost priceless. [Delete comma.]

Do not use a comma directly before or after a period, a question mark, an exclamation point, or a dash.

INCORRECT

"Were you late for work?", he asked. [Delete comma.]

With Parentheses

A comma may follow a closing parenthesis but may not come before an opening parenthesis.

CORRECT

After reading *The Color Purple* (written by Alice Walker), one better understands the cultural roots of black Americans.

Other Unnecessary Commas

* Do not use commas after coordinating conjunctions.

INCORRECT

We did not like the accommodations at the hotel, but, we found nothing else available. [Retain comma before *but;* delete comma after *but.*]

* A comma is not required after short adverbial modifiers.
  After a rain the desert blooms with wildflowers. [no comma required after *rain*]

* Do not use commas to set off restrictive clauses, phrases, or appositives.

INCORRECT

The water level, *at the lake,* is low. [restrictive prepositional phrase]

* Do not use a comma between adjectives that are cumulative and not co-ordinate. (See p. 180.)

INCORRECT

The new, Persian rug was beautiful. [Delete comma.]

13.1 Unnecessary Commas

■ *Circle all unnecessary commas in the following sentences.*

EXAMPLE

People⊘ who live in glass houses⊘ should not throw stones.

1. The ribbed vault, the flying buttress, and the pointed arch, characterize Gothic architecture.

2. Most popular lawn grasses, such as, fescue, centipede, and zoysia, are disease-resistant and drought-tolerant.

3. The investigator was surprised to find that the front door was locked, and that an alarm system had been installed.

4. Asphalt is one of many valuable petroleum byproducts, that have helped transform modern society.

5. Aberrations in Neptune's orbit, led to careful astronomical observations that confirmed the existence, of the planet Pluto.

6. The traffic was so heavy, that we left home thirty minutes earlier than we had planned.

7. The chemicals, that are frequently found in household cleaners like bleach and ammonia, can be very dangerous if mixed together.

8. The mayor of the city, and three members of the city council will hold a news conference tomorrow.

9. Since yesterday, the river, has risen two feet above flood stage.

10. Doctors, who do not wish to recommend back surgery, will frequently prescribe physical exercise instead.

13.2 Unnecessary Commas

■ *Circle all unnecessary commas in the following sentences.*

EXAMPLE
I am sure that the investment, was a wise one.

1. The new playground equipment, (a swing, monkey bars, and a slide) is very expensive, but, it comes with a thirty-year guarantee.

2. Over twenty-nine million copies, of *The Official Boy Scout Handbook,* have been sold, since its first edition was published in 1910.

3. Baz Luhrmann's, *Romeo and Juliet,* a modern version of Shakespeare's play, captures the mingled beauty, humor, and horror, of the original.

4. "Are you going home this weekend?", Elaine asked her roommate.

5. Sometimes, the cost of meals, purchased during business trips, can be deducted from taxable income.

6. In the American system of justice, a defendant is considered innocent, until proven guilty.

7. The centerpiece of the historic room was an original, Franklin stove.

8. With a little luck, the construction of the new hospital should be completed, before school begins, in the fall.

9. Our new piano will be delivered this week, possibly, by Wednesday.

10. The Coast Guard launch, skipped across the water, quickly slowed, and then turned, toward the pier.

NAME _____

DATE _____ SCORE _____

13.3 Unnecessary Commas: Review

■ *Circle the unnecessary commas in the following selection.*

The word *book,* comes from an Old English word, that means *tablet.*
Books are one of humanity's greatest inventions, because they allow people
to record and retrieve information. Over the centuries they have taken many
different forms. In ancient Babylon, scribes recorded business records, laws,
and stirring tales, like *The Epic of Gilgamesh,* on clay tablets. Of course, these
books, were heavy and cumbersome. At about the same time, Egyptians
were recording similar information on papyrus, a type of paper made from
reeds, that grew along the Nile River. They rolled sheets of papyrus on rods,
and the resulting scroll formed a lightweight, portable book. The Romans
made books even more durable and easy to use, by writing on treated animal skins, called parchment, and sewing the pages together. Called a *codex,*
this kind of book allowed readers to open directly to any page. Also, it was
more compact, because writers could use both sides of the sheet. The twentieth century witnessed another revolution, in bookmaking, with the advent
of electronic books. What would have filled a five-hundred-page codex,
might now fit on a 3.5-inch diskette. Furthermore, in this electronic format
books can be transported instantaneously, and keyword searches make it
possible to retrieve specific pieces of information, with only minimal effort.

14 Semicolons, Colons, Dashes, Parentheses, and Brackets

SEMICOLONS

Between Two Independent Clauses

- Use a semicolon between independent clauses not joined by *and, but, or, nor, for, so,* or *yet.* Remember, a semicolon should *not* be used between an independent and a dependent clause.

  In the 1950s, space flight was only a dream; in the 1960s, it was a reality.

- Use a semicolon before a conjunctive adverb that introduces an independent clause.

  Meredith and I removed the defective part; moreover, we sent a letter of complaint to the manufacturer.

- Use a semicolon to separate independent clauses that are long and complex or that have internal punctuation.

  Central City, located near Denver, was once a mining town in the nineteenth century; but since the decline of the mining industry, it has become noted for its summer opera program.

Between Items in a Series

- Use semicolons in a series between items that have internal punctuation (usually commas).

  In his closet Bill kept a photograph album, which was empty; several tennis shoes, all with holes in them; and the radiator cap from his first car, which he sold during his first year in college.

- Do not use a semicolon between elements that are not coordinate.

  INCORRECT

  After publishing *The Day of the Jackal* and several other popular novels; Frederick Forsyth wrote his most exciting book, *The Devil's Alternative.* [Use a comma, not a semicolon.]

COLONS

- Use a colon before quotations, statements, and series that are introduced formally.

  The geologist began his speech with a disturbing statement: "This country is short of rare metals."

- Use a colon to introduce a formal series.

>Bring the following items to the test: lined paper, two pencils, and a calculator.

Between Two Independent Clauses

Use a colon between two independent clauses when the second explains the first.

>Some car buyers base their decisions on a single criterion: does the dealership have a reputation for giving good service?

For Special Uses

Use the colon between hours and minutes.

>4:35 P.M.

Unnecessary Colon

Do not use a colon *after* a linking verb or a preposition.

INCORRECT

>Our best sales representatives are: Steven Walsh and Maria Moreno.

>Ron asked us to: list the items we needed, explain their use, and estimate their cost.

DASHES

Use dashes to introduce summaries or to show interruption, parenthetical comment, or special emphasis.

NOTE: On a typewriter or a word processor, a dash is formed by typing two hyphens.

For Summary

>Clothing, blankets, food, medicine—anything will help.

For Interruption

>Seven of my colleagues—I can't recall their names now—signed the petition.

For Parenthetical Comments

>This is important—at least to me—so listen carefully.

For Special Emphasis

The evidence points in only one direction—that of murder.

PARENTHESES

Use parentheses to enclose loosely related comments or explanations or to enclose numbers used to indicate items in a series.

That year (1950) was the happiest time of my life.

Please do the following: (1) fill out the form, (2) include a check or money order, and (3) list any special mailing instructions.

BRACKETS

Use brackets to enclose *interpolations*—that is, the writer's explanations— within a passage that is being quoted.

The senator objected: "I cannot agree with your [Senator Miner's] reasoning." [brackets used to set off writer's interpolation]

14.1 Semicolons

Use a semicolon between independent clauses not joined by a coordinating conjunction (*and, or, but, for, nor, so, yet*), before a conjunctive adverb that introduces another independent clause (*however, therefore, moreover, consequently,* etc.), and in a series between items that have internal punctuation (usually commas).

■ *Insert semicolons where they are needed in the following sentences. If necessary, cross out other marks of punctuation. Circle semicolons that you add.*

EXAMPLE

Tropical rain forests are incredibly luxuriant; they are, however, disappearing rapidly.

1. In 1900, the average life expectancy for an American was 47.3 years, by 1975, this average had increased to 72.4 years.

2. Matthew Brady's photographs of the Civil War provide a unique record of that war, they include glimpses of rest and recollection in addition to revealing the terrible aftermath of battle.

3. The Domesday Book is the oldest public record in Britain it was commissioned by William the Conqueror and completed in 1086.

4. Most people associate boomerangs with Australia, however, ancient boomerangs have been discovered in every inhabited continent except South America.

5. A group of whales is known as a *gam* a group of toads is called a *knot*.

6. Scientific prediction of earthquakes remains primitive and haphazard, nevertheless, scientists can make general predictions after monitoring magnetic charges along major faults.

7. Automatic transmission and air conditioning account for higher automotive fuel costs—for an eight-cylinder luxury car, the additional cost per ten thousand miles may reach $350, for a compact car, $250, and for a four-cylinder subcompact, $200.

8. Some specimens of the bristlecone pine are over 4,000 years old this extreme age makes them the oldest living things on Earth.

9. When parents look for good daycare, they must consider the reputation of the provider, the size, location, and quality of the facilities and the ratio of staff members to children.

10. The cutting edge of personal computer technology advances quickly and constantly PC owners who buy state-of-the-art machines today find them outdated almost as soon as the warranties expire.

14.2 Semicolons

■ *Insert semicolons where they are needed in the following sentences. If necessary, cross out other marks of punctuation. Circle semicolons that you add.*

NOTE: By using semicolons in this way, you can eliminate comma splices and fused sentences.

EXAMPLE
The project was time-consuming (;) it lasted a week longer than scheduled.

1. The first wedding guests to arrive were quite perplexed they found the church door locked and on the door a sign that read "Closed for Repair."

2. Hot-air balloons fill the skies near Albuquerque, New Mexico, every fall, thousands of enthusiasts flock to the city to enjoy the sight.

3. New Year's Eve celebrations include fireworks and champagne traditionally revelers also sing at least one stanza of "Auld Lang Syne."

4. Czar Peter the Great was a tall man, indeed he stood nearly seven feet tall.

5. Many Americans assume that New York City is the busiest U.S. port, New Orleans, however, actually holds that distinction.

6. When purchasing an automobile battery, the consumer should compare various brands and sizes, standards of comparison may include a battery's cold-cranking power, reserve capacity, ampere-hour capacity, and total number of plates.

7. The most highly paid butlers, whose annual salaries exceed $50,000, are knowledgeable about food, wine, and formal etiquette capable of managing and supervising large household staffs and gifted with discreet, diplomatic temperaments.

8. Baseball is still the most popular Little League sport in America, soccer, however, is the fastest-growing.

9. The Latin American country of Costa Rica has more native plant species than all of North America, furthermore, the plants are highly concentrated in a relatively small geographical area.

10. The hustle and bustle of pre-holiday traffic can be aggravating, a growing number of shoppers prefer browsing through mail-order catalogs to orbiting jammed parking lots.

14.3 Colons and Dashes

Use a **colon** before quotations, statements, and series that are introduced formally. A colon also may be used between two independent clauses when the second explains the first. Use a **dash** to introduce summaries or to show interpretation, parenthetical comment, or special emphasis.

■ *Correctly punctuate the following sentences. Circle punctuation that you add. Write* **C** *to the right of any sentence that is correct.*

EXAMPLES

All of New England⊝Connecticut, Maine, Massachusetts, New Hampshire, Rhode Island, and Vermont⊝is likely to suffer serious fuel shortages during bad winters.

The process of writing entails these steps⊙prewriting, drafting, and revision.

1. The first speaker described one phenomenon jogging that she believes reflects many contemporary values of society.

2. Many theaters find that an 815 curtain time means fewer latecomers than one at 800.

3. Several features narrow handmade tires, sophisticated derailleurs, and lightweight alloy framing distinguish modern racing bicycles.

4. Most accidents have a single cause carelessness.

5. Marcus remembered reading only one worthwhile book during his summer vacation Ralph Ellison's *Invisible Man*.

6. Before the 1600s, all carrots were one of three colors red, purple, or black.

7. The most common means of evaluation the intelligence test is no longer considered sufficient as the sole reason for placement in special classes.

8. Altricial birds woodpeckers, songbirds, and hummingbirds, for instance are blind and almost featherless at birth.

9. After the FAA completed its examination of the wreckage, it concluded that there could be only one reason for the crash pilot error.

10. Halfway down the page, the following admonition appeared in bold print DO NOT WRITE BELOW THIS LINE.

14.4 Parentheses and Brackets

Use **parentheses** to enclose loosely related comments or explanations or to enclose numbers used to indicate items in a series. Use **brackets** to enclose *interpolations*—that is, the writer's explanations—within a passage that is being quoted.

■ *Insert parentheses and brackets where they are needed in the following sentences. Circle parentheses and brackets that you add.*

EXAMPLE
One type of blueberry (the rabbit-eye) is native to the Deep South.

1. The Gross National Product GNP refers to the total value of goods and services a country produces in a year.

2. Saint Valentine's Day February 14 is observed in honor of a Christian martyr.

3. The Hermitage, home of President Andrew Jackson, is about ten miles 16 kilometers from downtown Nashville, Tennessee.

4. The agronomist considered soybeans the crop of the future because 1 they are hearty, 2 they are high in protein, and 3 they require relatively little expensive fertilizer.

5. Descriptions may be *objective* focusing on the object itself or *subjective* focusing on an individual's response to the object.

6. The coded message read, "Tell the Boss Senator Butler that the Eagle the German ambassador has landed."

7. The major regions of Germany include 1 the Northern Plain, 2 the Central Highlands, and 3 the South German Hills.

8. "This *stele* a commemorative stone tablet dates from the eighth century B.C.," said the museum guide.

9. Some options for savers mutual funds, tax-exempt bonds, and zero-coupon bonds are imperfectly understood by many consumers.

10. "That was the year 1965," he said, "when we planned to expand our market to include the West Coast."

15 Quotation Marks and End Punctuation

QUOTATION MARKS

- Use quotation marks to enclose the exact words of a speaker or writer.

    "I'm glad you came," she said. [declarative statement and object of verb *said*]

    "Turn in your papers," he demanded. [command]

    "Have you already finished?" she asked. [question]

    "Look out!" he cried. [exclamation]

- *Periods* and *commas* always are placed inside quotation marks. *Semicolons* and *colons* always are placed outside quotation marks. *Question marks* and *exclamation points* are placed inside quotation marks when they refer to the quotation itself. They are placed outside the quotation marks when they refer to the entire sentence.

    Who said, "We need a new car"? [Quotation is a statement.]

- Use quotation marks to enclose dialogue. Do not use quotation marks with indirect quotations.

    Alexander Pope once wrote, "A little learning is a dangerous thing." [direct quotation]

    Alexander Pope said that a little learning can be dangerous. [indirect quotation]

- In dialogue a new paragraph marks each change of speaker.

    "Do you have change for a dollar?" the customer asked after searching in his pocket for change.

    "I think so," replied the cashier.

Quotation Within a Quotation

Use single quotation marks to enclose a quotation within a quotation.

    "I do not know what you mean when you say, 'Improve your extension,'" complained the novice skater.

Titles

Use quotation marks to enclose the titles of essays, articles, short stories, chapters, television programs that are not series, and short musical compositions.

We enjoy reading William Safire's column, "On Language," in the Sunday newspaper. [article in newspaper]

The band began to play Sousa's "Stars and Stripes Forever." [short musical composition]

Unnecessary Quotation Marks

Do not use quotation marks to emphasize or change the usual meanings of words or to point out the use of slang or attempts at humor. If you must use such language, let it stand without comment.

INCORRECT

We had a "great" time at the party. [emphasis]

That movie was really "bad." [change of meaning]

I guess we "goofed." [slang]

His lemonades are so bad that they always turn out to be "lemons." [attempted humor]

END PUNCTUATION

- Use a period after sentences that make statements and after sentences that express a command that is not exclamatory.

  The restaurant is crowded. [statement]

  Call me in the morning. [mild command]

- Use a question mark after a direct question.

  How long have you been waiting?

- Use an exclamation point after a word, a phrase, or a sentence to indicate strong feeling.

  Ouch! That hurt!

  Stop that man!

- Remember to use a period after mild exclamations.

  That is the craziest idea I ever heard.

15.1 Quotation Marks and End Punctuation

■ *Correctly punctuate the following sentences. Circle any incorrect punctuation and indicate what punctuation should be used. Indicate a new paragraph with the sign ¶.*

EXAMPLE

"Where do we keep these files," asked the manager With the Smith account, replied her secretary.

1. Where was Patrick Henry when he said Give me liberty or give me death?

2. Remarkable and outstanding was the phrase one observer used to describe the relief agency's efforts in the war-ravaged country.

3. English poet William Blake wrote I must Create a System or be enslaved by another Man's.

4. After stepping on the moon, Neil Armstrong remarked, One small step for (a) man; one giant leap for mankind.

5. The chorus began its Fourth of July concert with America, the Beautiful.

6. Ernest Hemingway's short story A Very Short Story concerns the relationship between a wounded American soldier and an attractive Spanish nurse.

7. When you have finished reading the paper, asked her husband, may I have the sports section?

8. Yes, Virginia, there is a Santa Claus is perhaps the most widely read editorial in the history of the *New York Sun.*

9. The press corps wondered what exactly the role of the president's science adviser would be.

10. Did you know that some of the officers in the American Revolution came to this country from Poland specifically to help us win the war asked the history instructor. Our town, Pulaski, Tennessee, is named for one of them a student answered. Correct that was Count Casimir Pulaski responded the teacher.

15.2 Quotation Marks and End Punctuation

■ *Correctly punctuate the following sentences. Circle any incorrect punctuation. Indicate a new paragraph with the sign ¶.*

EXAMPLE
The referee's cry, "Stop! You are out of bounds!" was lost in the noise of the crowd.

1. The article's title, The Ethics of Price Fixing, is sure to stimulate response.

2. To freeze peaches droned the television chef use citric acid to prevent the fruit from turning brown.

3. Once hopelessly outdated, big bands are now considered "cool," even "hot."

4. When does spring break begin this year, asked Mandy?

5. Who said, "The only place where he would be the life of the party is in a mortuary!"

6. Look out! he exclaimed; the cable is about to snap!

7. Why do good people have to suffer, the minister asked?

8. Do you know whether Stevie Ray Vaughn ever performed the Jimi Hendrix song Little Wing.

9. The novel's first chapter, A Tortuous Beginning, was so confusing that I refused to continue reading.

10. What time is it? Kim asked. I don't know, Derrick replied. Has the alarm already gone off, she asked. I didn't hear it, he said.

Mechanics

16 Underlining for Italics

Underline titles of books (except the Bible and its divisions), periodicals, newspapers, motion pictures, television series, long musical compositions (operas and symphonies, for example), works of art, plays, and works published separately, and occasionally, words to be emphasized.

TITLES

Books

> The World Almanac

Periodicals

> U.S. News & World Report

Newspapers

> Washington Post or Washington Post

Motion Pictures and Television Series

> Psycho
>
> Masterpiece Theatre

Long Musical Compositions, Paintings, and Sculpture

> Handel's Messiah
>
> Rodin's The Thinker

Plays

> Hamlet

NAMES OF SHIPS, TRAINS, AND OTHER VEHICLES

Underline the names of ships and trains.

> The USS Nimitz
>
> the Zephyr
>
> the space shuttle Columbia

FOREIGN WORDS

Underline foreign words used in an English context if they have not become a part of our language. Check the dictionary before underlining foreign words.

Like Americans, Brazilians love soap operas, which they call <u>telenovelas</u>.

WORDS BEING NAMED

Underline words, letters, and figures being named.

The word <u>effigy</u> comes from the Latin term for image.

Be sure to cross your <u>t</u>s.

FOR OCCASIONAL EMPHASIS

Although underlining for emphasis is permissible on occasion, avoid excessive underlining because it often reveals a writer's weak vocabulary.

NOT

That is not just a big dinner. That is a <u>big</u> dinner.

IMPROVED

That is not just a big dinner. That is a feast.

16.1 Italics

■ *Underline for italics in the following sentences.*

EXAMPLE

The <u>Verdict</u> is a superb movie about modern journalism.

1. Unlike other newspapers, USA Today is distributed nationwide.

2. Lorry is the British word for truck.

3. People learning to pronounce English as a foreign language often find ls, gs, and ks to be troublesome.

4. The New Yorker is as famous for its cartoons as for its articles and reviews of art, literature, and drama.

5. Gabriel García Márquez, a Colombian-born, Nobel Prize–winning novelist, wrote One Hundred Years of Solitude.

6. The common abbreviation A.M. stands for ante meridiem, a Latin phrase meaning "before noon."

7. The Soviet Union launched Sputnik I, the world's first artificial satellite, in 1957.

8. For more than two hundred years, George Frederick Handel's Messiah has been a favorite piece of Christmas music.

9. J. M. Barrie wrote the play Peter Pan specifically for children.

10. Cat on a Hot Tin Roof signaled a new direction in Elizabeth Taylor's movie career.

16.2 Italics

■ *Underline for italics in the following sentences.*

EXAMPLE

<u>Audubon: A Vision</u> is a long poem by Robert Penn Warren.

1. The United States, not the Queen Elizabeth II, was the largest ocean liner ever built.

2. Mario Lloso Vargas, a noted Peruvian novelist, wrote Conversations in the Cathedral.

3. Edith Wharton's novel The Age of Innocence, first published in 1920, was made into a successful film in 1993.

4. The wat, or Buddhist temple, serves as the social and religious center of most Thai villages.

5. American writer Robert Penn Warren won a Pulitzer Prize for his novel All the King's Men and also served as poet laureate.

6. A roman à clef is a novel that, like Thomas Wolfe's Look Homeward, Angel, presents real people and events under fictional names.

7. Movies like Stand Up and Cheer, The Littlest Rebel, and Dimples made Shirley Temple the most popular child star of the 1930s.

8. The sinking of the Titanic continues to haunt the public imagination.

9. Ishmael Reed's novel Mumbo Jumbo retells the history of the United States from an unusual, provocative, and highly entertaining perspective.

10. The Washington Post is the only newspaper published in Washington, D.C.

17 Spelling

Spell correctly. Use a dictionary when you are uncertain of the spelling of a word.

Be particularly careful with words that are not spelled as they sound (*though* and *debt*), words that sound the same (*sew* and *so*), and words with the "uh" sound, which gives no clue to their spelling (*terrible* and *persistent*).

Do not misspell words by omitting a syllable that is occasionally and erroneously not pronounced (*accidently* for *accidentally*), by adding syllables (*mischievious* for *mischievous*), or by changing syllables (*preform* for *perform*).

GUIDES FOR SPELLING

For *ie* and *ei*

Use *i* before *e* (*believe*) except after *c* (*receive*) or when these letters are sounded as *a* (*neighbor*). There are a few exceptions (*either, neither, leisure, seize, weird, height*).

Final *e*

Drop the final *e* when adding a **suffix** if the suffix begins with a vowel (*dine* to *dining*). Keep the *e* if the suffix begins with a consonant (*improve* to *improvement*). There are some exceptions (for example, *judge* becomes *judgment*, *notice* becomes *noticeable*, and *awe* becomes *awful*).

For Changing *y* to *i*

Change the *y* to *i* when the *y* is preceded by a consonant but not when the *y* is preceded by a vowel or when *-ing* is added (*story* becomes *stories, delay* becomes *delays*, and *fly* becomes *flying*).

Suffixes

If a suffix begins with a consonant, do not double the final consonant of a word (*quick* becomes *quickly*). If the suffix begins with a vowel, double the last consonant of one-syllable words (*bat* becomes *batting*) and of words of more than one syllable if the accent is on the last syllable (*occur'* becomes *occurrence*). Do not double the final consonant if that consonant is preceded by two vowels (*repair* becomes *repairing*), if the word ends with two or more consonants (*drink* becomes *drinking*), or if the last syllable of the word is not stressed after the suffix is added (*prefer'* becomes *pref'erence*).

Plurals

Add -s for plurals of most nouns (*sound* becomes *sounds*) and for nouns ending in *o* when it is preceded by a vowel (*portfolio* becomes *portfolios*). Add -es when the plural has another syllable that is pronounced (*speech* becomes *speeches*) and in most cases when the noun ends in *o* preceded by a consonant (*tomato* becomes *tomatoes*). See a dictionary for the exceptions.

The plurals of proper names are generally formed by adding -s or -es (*Taylor, Taylors; Jones, Joneses*). The plurals of letters and numbers are formed by adding an *s*. Do not add an apostrophe except when it is necessary to avoid confusion. ("The word *insinuate* has two *i*'s.") In compound words, add the *s* in the most logical place. (Speakers of the House, Checkbooks).

240

NAME _____

DATE _____ SCORE _____

17.1 Suffixes

■ *In the blank spaces provided, write the correct spellings of the following word and suffix combinations.*

EXAMPLES

cite / ing _____ *citing* _____

judge / ment _____ *judgment* _____

1. mobile / ity _____

2. equip / ing _____

3. domestic / ate _____

4. notice / able _____

5. pat / ed _____

6. forbid / en _____

7. necessary / ly _____

8. use / age _____

9. neutral / ity _____

10. real / istic _____

11. wake / ing _____

12. like / able _____

13. believe / able _____

14. interchange / able _____

15. contaminate / ing _____

16. beauty / eous _____

17. commit / ing _____

18. cram / ed _____

19. defy / ance _____

20. hinge / ing _____

21. fry / ed _____

22. fry / ing _____

23. lose / ing _____

24. fret / ed _____

25. cancel / ed _____

26. house / ing _____

27. offense / less _____

28. defer / ed _____

29. control / ing _____

30. receive / able _____

NAME _____

DATE _____ SCORE _____

17.2 Suffixes

■ *In the blank spaces provided, write the correct spellings of the following word and suffix combinations.*

EXAMPLES

stop / ing _____ *stopping* _____

exhaust / tion _____ *exhaustion* _____

1. tap / ed _____

2. accrue / ing _____

3. pry / ing _____

4. possible / ity _____

5. flex / ible _____

6. dine / ing _____

7. versatile / ity _____

8. lone / liness _____

9. domesticate / tion _____

10. envy / able _____

11. forget / ing _____

12. omit / ed _____

13. assume / ing _____

14. prescribe / ing _____

15. cast / ing _____

16. marvel / ous _____

17. deny / ing _____

18. adequate / ly _____

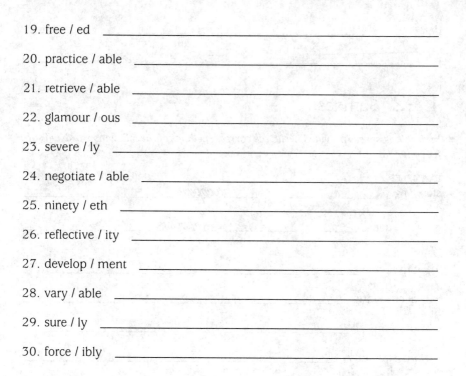

19. free / ed _____

20. practice / able _____

21. retrieve / able _____

22. glamour / ous _____

23. severe / ly _____

24. negotiate / able _____

25. ninety / eth _____

26. reflective / ity _____

27. develop / ment _____

28. vary / able _____

29. sure / ly _____

30. force / ibly _____

17.3 Spelling with *ie* and *ei*

■ *Fill in the blanks in the following words with* **ie** *or* **ei**.

EXAMPLES
defic _ie_ nt

v _ei_ n

1. consc_____nce

2. p_____ce

3. conc_____t

4. h_____ght

5. forf_____t

6. rec_____ve

7. qu_____t

8. gr_____f

9. dec_____t

10. p_____rce

11. misch_____vous

12. fr_____ght

13. pat_____nce

14. fr_____nd

15. n_____ce

16. for_____gn

17. inconven_____nt

18. trans_____nt

19. s_____ge

20. bel_____

21. anx_____ty

22. rec_____pt

23. sal_____nt

24. inv_____gh

25. len_____nt

26. perc_____ve

27. r_____ns

28. resil_____nt

29. ineffic_____nt

30. th_____f

NAME _____

DATE _____ SCORE _____

17.4 Spelling with *ie* and *ei*

■ *Fill in the blanks in the following words with* **ie** *or* **ei**.

EXAMPLES
prem _*ie*_ r

st _*ei*_ n

1. sl_____gh

2. f_____ld

3. retr_____ve

4. ch_____f

5. gr_____vance

6. w_____rd

7. rec_____ve

8. v_____l

9. rev_____w

10. h_____r

11. p_____ce

12. cash_____r

13. n_____ghbor

14. l_____sure

15. sc_____nce

16. surv_____llance

17. h_____nous

18. bel_____ve

19. forf_____t

20. bes_____ge

21. ach_____ve

22. shr_____k

23. mil_____u

24. t_____r

25. br_____f

26. _____ght

27. rel_____f

28. w_____gh

29. s_____zure

30. w_____ld

17.5 Plurals

■ *Form the plural for each of the following nouns. If there is more than one plural form, give all of them. Consult your dictionary when in doubt.*

EXAMPLES

bush _____ *bushes* _____

piano _____ *pianos* _____

1. Williams _____

2. money _____

3. cactus _____

4. bastion _____

5. bureaucracy _____

6. basis _____

7. corona _____

8. syllabus _____

9. antenna _____

10. oasis _____

11. phenomenon _____

12. half _____

13. attorney _____

14. memorandum _____

15. beau _____

16. mother-in-law _____

17. essay _____

18. envelope _____

19. embargo _____

20. crisis _____

21. volley _____

22. alumnus _____

23. index _____

24. medium _____

25. criterion _____

26. zero _____

27. radius _____

28. axis _____

29. flash _____

30. rice _____

18 Hyphenation and Syllabication

Use a hyphen in certain compound words and in words divided at the end of a line.

It is best to consult a dictionary to determine whether a compound word is hyphenated or is written as one or two words. Hyphenate a compound of two or more words used as a single modifier before a noun.

HYPHEN

He is a *well-known* millionaire.

NO HYPHEN

The millionaire is *well known.*

Hyphenate spelled-out compound numbers from *twenty-one* through *ninety-nine.*

When hyphenating a word at the end of a line, do not divide one-syllable words (*m-en,* for example), do not put a one-letter syllable on a separate line (*a-long,* for example), and avoid carrying over a two-letter suffix to another line (*relat-ed*). Divide words according to the syllabication in the dictionary.

NOT

re-cluse

BUT

rec-luse

NAME _____

DATE _____ SCORE _____

18.1 Hyphenation and Syllabication

■ *Write the correct spelling of the following compounds in the blanks at the right. If a spelling is correct, write C in the blank. Consult a dictionary.*

EXAMPLES

hat-less *hatless*

reenter *re-enter*

1. road-side _____

2. waiting-list _____

3. software _____

4. fifty five _____

5. rattle snake _____

6. tough minded _____

7. one-hundred _____

8. uni-lateral _____

9. nation wide _____

10. laissez faire _____

11. down-stream _____

12. one-twelfth _____

13. a freelance artist _____

14. babysit _____

15. per cent _____

16. a nimbostratus cloud _____

17. a six question form _____

18. ice cream cone _____

19. long-distance telephone call   _____

20. great grandmother   _____

21. free loader   _____

22. all-purpose flour   _____

23. ultra-modern   _____

24. excouncilor   _____

25. a do-it-yourself project   _____

26. teen-ager   _____

27. post-war   _____

28. a deepseated habit   _____

29. a day-care center   _____

30. a highschool   _____

18.2 Hyphenation and Syllabication

■ *Circle errors in hyphenation or syllabication and correct them. Add hyphens where necessary.*

EXAMPLE

The⊖once-popular convertible is again on the market.

1. The cashier short-changed the customer.

2. The Spanish speaking nations of North America include many different

   ethnic groups.

3. A troubleshooter came from the maintenance department.

4. The Bill-of-Rights outlines the freedom guaranteed all Americans.

5. The children spent all morning in their play-house.

6. Physicians warn that quack remedies for arthritis—apple-cider, vinegar,

   a dry-climate, or a copper-bracelet—have no medical value.

7. My twelve hour flight resulted in a real case of jet lag.

8. Some political theorists believe that the attorney-general should be in-

   dependent of the White-House, and a congressional subcommittee is

   studying this suggestion.

9. The low mark-up makes this shirt a best-seller.

10. Twenty-seven of the fifteen hundred Tshirts were defective.

19 Apostrophes, Capital Letters, Abbreviations, and Numbers

APOSTROPHES

- Use the apostrophe for the possessive case of many nouns, for contractions and omissions, and for some plurals.

- Use 's for the possessive of nouns not ending in *s*.

SINGULAR	PLURAL
book's, Albert's	people's, children's

- Use 's or ' without the *s* for the possessive of singular nouns ending in *s*. Do not add the *s* when a singular noun ending in *s* is followed by a word that begins with *s*.

  Dennis's, or Dennis' *but not* Dennis's stories

- Use ' without the *s* to form the possessive of plural nouns ending in *s*.

  the Wilsons' mailbox, the players' strategies

- Use 's to form the possessive of indefinite pronouns.

  anyone's, everybody's, neither's

- Use 's with only the last noun when indicating joint possession in a pair or series.

  Michael and Sherri's wedding was beautiful. [They share the wedding.]
  Michael's and Sherri's parents attended. [They do not share parents.]

- Use ' to show omissions or to form contractions.

  won't, it's [it is]

CAPITAL LETTERS

- Use a capital letter to begin a sentence and to designate a proper noun. Capitalize the first word in a sentence, the letter *I,* and the interjection *O.*

  What, O what, have I done?

- Capitalize the first, last, and important words in titles, including the second part of hyphenated words.

  Great Expectations
  The Man with the Golden Horn
  Slaughterhouse-Five

- Capitalize first words in quotations and words capitalized by the author.

  "We could call this the Age of Indifference," the author wrote.

- Capitalize titles preceding names.

  Lord Mountbatten

- Capitalize the title of the head of a nation even when the name of the person is not given. Capitalize titles that substitute for specific names.

  The Prime Minister is in conference.

  General Ames has been in Europe. The General has been inspecting NATO units.

- A title not followed by a name is usually not capitalized.

  The secretary read the minutes of the last meeting.

- Titles that are common nouns naming an office are not capitalized.

  A private has a hard life.

- Capitalize degrees and titles after names.

  Bill Davis, Director of Admissions

  Martha Blount, C.P.A.

- Capitalize words of family relationships used as names when not preceded by a possessive pronoun.

  Have you seen Mom?

- Capitalize proper nouns and their derivatives.

  Paris, Parisian; the Southwest; Democrats, the Democratic Party; the Missouri River; Middle Atlantic States

- Capitalize movements, periods, and events in history.

  the Romantic Movement, the Civil War

- Capitalize words referring to deities, to religious denominations, and to religious literature. Pronouns referring to deities are usually capitalized.

  God, Methodism, the Bible, Allah, the Koran

  We know He is our God.

- Capitalize the titles of specific courses and the names of languages.

  Biology 126, Music 240

  Mathematics 101 *but* a mathematics course [because not specific]

ABBREVIATIONS

- Avoid most abbreviations in writing. Spell out the names of days, months, units of measurement, and (except in addresses) states and countries. In addresses use the abbreviations of the U.S. Postal Service (NY, CA, TX).

    Monday [*not* Mon.]; February [*not* Feb.]; ounce [*not* oz.]; Fort Worth, Texas [*not* TX]

- Abbreviations are acceptable before names (Mr., Dr.), after names (Sr., D.D.S.), and with dates and time (B.C., A.D. and A.M., P.M.).

NUMBERS

- Spell out numbers that can be written in one word or two words. Do not spell out years.

    thirty-two
    two million
    1991

- Use figures for other numbers.

    12,367, $978.34, 3⅓

- Never begin sentences with figures. Rephrase the sentence or spell the numbers out.

NOT

50 men started work.

BUT

Fifty men started work.

- Use numerals for figures in a series.

    We bought 10 pounds of potatoes, 2 quarts of milk, and 2 dozen eggs.

- Use figures for dates, street numbers, page references, percentages, and hours of the day used with A.M. or P.M.

USE FIGURES	SPELL OUT
March 7, 1981	the seventh of March
4511 Mary Ellen Avenue	Tenth Street
See page 10.	The book has twenty pages.
He paid 10 percent interest.	
The meeting starts at 10 P.M.	The meeting starts at ten o'clock.

19.1 Apostrophes

Use the apostrophe for the possessive case of many nouns, for contractions and omissions, and for some plurals.

■ *Give the singular possessive and the plural possessive of the following nouns.*

EXAMPLE
campaign _____*campaign's*_____ _____*campaigns'*_____

	SINGULAR POSSESSIVE	PLURAL POSSESSIVE
1. city		
2. wife		
3. sprinkler		
4. video		
5. university		
6. Burris (last name)		
7. genius		
8. visitor		
9. druggist		
10. spectator		
11. relative		
12. cemetery		
13. copy		
14. girl		
15. Liu (last name)		
16. knife		
17. Mathis (last name)		

	SINGULAR POSSESSIVE	PLURAL POSSESSIVE
18. society		
19. father-in-law		
20. Roberts (last name)		
21. baby		
22. monkey		
23. leaf		
24. zoo		
25. scientist		

19.2 Apostrophes

Use the apostrophe for the possessive case of many nouns, for contractions and omissions, and for some plurals.

■ *Add apostrophes where necessary and circle incorrect apostrophes. Change spellings where appropriate.*

EXAMPLES

Most people's opinions are based on feelings, not facts. [Apostrophe precedes the *s* because *people* is plural.]

Roger often complained about the demand's of his busy schedule. [*demand* is not possessive.]

1. Hundreds of toy's built on our main plants assembly line were returned because they were defective.

2. Many residents' of Miami, Florida, still remember the hurricane that destroyed or damaged hundreds of homes' in the area.

3. Marty worked on his research paper from eight oclock until midnight.

4. *Vanguard I,* an early satellite, was launched in 1958, but its not scheduled to reenter Earths atmosphere for 600 years.

5. For most Americans, the 1980s' and 1990s' were times of prosperity.

6. Most of an attorneys day—from eight oclock until two oclock—is spent in hearings, committee meetings, and court sessions.

7. Romes last emperor was overthrown in 476 B.C.

8. The Smith's were invited to the Jones' house for a party welcoming the Davises'.

9. The alligator whipped it's tail toward the mens' boat.

10. My favorite mechanics estimate was lower than that of either one of his competitors, so I let him rebuild the transmission.

19.3 Capitals

Use a capital letter to begin a sentence and to designate a proper noun.

■ *Circle and correct the errors in capitalization.*

EXAMPLE
Health-Conscious Americans are eating more Frozen Yogurt and less Ice Cream.

1. The empire state building in New York City was once the world's tallest skyscraper.

2. Pictures like *el jaleo, lady with a rose, and gassed* helped make John Singer Sargent one of the most popular painters of the early Twentieth Century.

3. Over 700 years ago, the anasazi people of the American southwest built cliff dwellings that continue to amaze visitors today.

4. My roommate Muhammad was born in north Carolina.

5. The prime minister met with king Faisal for several hours at 10 Downing street.

6. American tourists frequently confuse canadian coins with their U.S. counterparts.

7. On January 4, 1973, representatives of several major businesses met in san francisco to develop the Bar Code used today at virtually every checkout counter.

8. Margaret Atwood, Poet and Novelist, wrote the Best-selling Novel *The handmaid's tale.*

9. Eric Arthur Blair, known to the Public as George Orwell, was a British Essayist who satirized modern politicians for their use of such phrases as *render inoperative, militate against, make contact with, be subjected to,* and *make itself felt.*

10. Near Seattle washington is one of north America's last surviving rain forests, the hoh Rain Forest.

19.4 Abbreviations and Numbers

Avoid most **abbreviations** in writing. Spell out the names of days, months, units of measurement, and states and countries. Remember to use the abbreviations of the U.S. Postal Service for states in addresses. Spell out **numbers** that can be written in one word or two words. Never begin a sentence with a number (or figure). Use numerals for figures in a series and use figures for dates, street numbers, page references, percentages, and hours of the day used with A.M. or P.M.

■ *Correct unacceptable usage of abbreviations and numbers. Write corrections above the line.*

EXAMPLE *forty and*
We caught 40 fish & sailed for home.

1. The Chattahoochee River supplies 300 million gal. of water each day to the greater Atlanta area before flowing south into the Gulf of Mexico.

2. 2,000 calories a day is common in diets designed for active males.

3. The Kiwanis Club will hold its next fundraiser on March fifteenth.

4. The Metro. Transit Authority purchased 22 new buses for two million, four hundred forty thousand dollars.

5. A good recipe for yeast rolls appears on page 9 of her latest cookbook.

6. One lineman weighed two hundred fifty lbs.; another, two hundred forty lbs.; the third, two hundred sixty lbs.; and the last, two hundred eighty lbs.—all for an average weight of 257 pt. 5 lbs.

7. 1,000,000 fewer people lived in Chicago in 1990 than in 1950, according to census figures.

8. Retail sales rose over 12.5% between Oct. & Dec.

9. On the 25th day of Nov., many Eng. composition courses met for the last time.

10. The Rev. Mr. Smith, Sen. Martinez, and Capt. Briggs of the A.F. were present for the commissioning of the new Lts.

19.5 Capitals, Abbreviations, and Numbers: Review

■ *Correct all errors in capitalization, abbreviations, and the use of numbers in the following paragraph.*

One of the greatest dangers facing space travelers today is a swarm of human-made particles orbiting the earth. 106 particles struck the space shuttle *columbia* on a recent mission. In an effort to avoid these dangerous projectiles, the U.S. space command, located in Colorado Springs, CO, tracks every piece of space junk that is any larger than two-and-one-half inches in diameter. At present, there are about 9,000 pieces of debris this size in orbit around the earth. Some of these are moving dangerously fast, up to 17,000 m.p.h. At this speed, a projectile that weighs one oz. can create an 18-in. hole in a sheet of steel that is 1 inch thick. Researchers continue to work on better armor plating for spacecraft, but avoiding contact with the deadly particles is the best way to avoid disaster.

Adapted from James R. Chiles, "Casting a High-Tech Net for Space Junk,"
Smithsonian 29, no. 10 (1999): 46–55.

19.6 Apostrophes, Capitals, Abbreviations, and Numbers: Review

- *Correct all errors in apostrophes, capitalization, abbreviations, and the use of numbers in the following paragraph.*

Under an ancient calendar, the Roman's observed March 25, the beginning of spring, as the first day of the year. Emperors and high-ranking officials, though, repeatedly tampered with the length of months and years to extend their terms of office. Calendar dates were so desynchronized with astronomical benchmarks by the year 153 B.C. that the roman senate, to set many public occasions straight, declared the start of the New Year as Jan. 1. More tampering again set dates askew. To reset the calendar to Jan. 1 in forty-six B.C., Julius Caesar had to let the year drag on for 445 days, earning it the historical sobriquet "Year of Confusion." Caesars new calendar was eponymously called the julian calendar.

Charles Panati, Extraordinary Origins of Everyday Things
(New York: Harper, 1987), 46–47.

Diction and Style

20 Standard English and Style

THE DICTIONARY

Dictionaries contain information that is necessary for precise writing. The following entry from the *American Heritage Dictionary* for the word *bureaucrat* indicates the kinds of information that are found in an entry. The numbers in brackets have been added.

> **bu·reau·crat** [1] (byoor′ə-krăt′) [2] *n.* [3] 1. An official of a bureaucracy. 2. Any official who insists on rigid adherence to rules, forms, and routines. [4]—**bu′reau·crat′ic** *adj.*—**bu′reau·crat′i·cal·ly** *adv.* [5] **Usage:** In American usage *bureaucrat* is almost invariably derogatory unless the context establishes otherwise.

After the entry word, which is divided into syllables, you will find the following information: (1) the pronunciation of the word, (2) the part of speech, (3) the definitions of the word, (4) the ways the word is spelled for other parts of speech, and (5) the way the word is used.

Dictionaries also include the following:

1. Principal parts of regular and irregular verbs
2. Archaic forms of inflected verbs (*dost* for the second-person present tense of *do*)
3. Plurals of nouns
4. Irregular forms of nouns
5. Comparative and superlative degrees of adjectives and adverbs
6. Labels for the technical or limited use of words (*chemistry* or *sports,* for example)
7. Other labels indicating restricted usage (*nonstandard, slang, poetic, foreign languages*)
8. Cross-references to other words and spelling variations
9. Etymologies
10. Synonyms
11. Standard abbreviations
12. Miscellaneous information, including references to famous people, to geographic areas, and to important historical movements and periods

USAGE

Standard English is the accepted language of English-speaking people. In formal writing, avoid using informal words. Replace nonstandard words in most kinds of prose. Read the labels in a current dictionary.

NOT

She was fired up about her new job.

BUT

She was excited about her new job.

IMPROPRIETIES

Improprieties are the uses of words as the wrong parts of speech or the incorrect uses of words for similar words that have different meanings.

IMPROPRIETY	PROPER FORM
ice tea [noun for adjective]	iced tea
easy understood [adjective for adverb]	easily understood
a quite morning	a quiet morning
new personal	new personnel

IDIOMS

Idioms are accepted expressions with meanings that differ from the meanings of the individual words themselves.

Sometimes my sister drives me up a wall. [irritates me]

Many idioms are incorrect because the wrong prepositions are used.

INCORRECT	CORRECT
conform with	conform to
oblivious to	oblivious of
in reference with	in reference to
the year of 1999	the year 1999

TRITENESS

Triteness includes worn-out or hackneyed phrases and figures of speech. Substitutes that are fresh and original should be used. Avoid such expressions as the following:

best and brightest	to each his own
rhyme or reason	last but not least
time will tell	one in a million

EXACTNESS

Correct usage requires a knowledge of idioms, the use of a current dictionary, and wide experience with words. Words must be used precisely; writers should avoid using words that are confusing or vague.

Many people today diet in an effort to become *lanky*. [A better choice would be *slender*.]

He was in difficult *straights*. [The word should be *straits*, meaning a difficult situation.]

20.1 The Dictionary and Usage

■ *Look up each word in parentheses in a current dictionary to determine the correct choice. Underline the answer and write a summary of the statement about usage given in the dictionary.*

EXAMPLE

The television (<u>medium</u>, media) has benefited greatly from satellite broadcasting.

medium; refers to one kind of communication method

media; plural form for more than one kind

1. My grandmother promised to call me (sometime, some time) next week.

   _____

   _____

2. (Since, Being as) a knee injury ruined his chances of being selected early in the professional draft, Alberto decided to attend graduate school.

   _____

   _____

3. Studying with students from backgrounds (different from, different than) our own can be very enlightening.

   _____

   _____

4. We plan to go to the movies (if, whether) the rain has stopped or not.

   _____

   _____

5. The (criterion, criteria) for a successful defense lawyer might be surprising to some: legal expertise and calmness under pressure, certainly, but equally the common touch so that a jury will see the lawyer as a real person.

_____

_____

6. Shakespeare asks in one of his sonnets whether he should compare his love (to, with) a summer's day.

_____

_____

7. (Regardless, Irregardless) of his questionable political beliefs, Ezra Pound remains an important twentieth-century poet.

_____

_____

8. Credit card offers fall into several (discrete, discreet) categories.

_____

_____

9. Almost everyone in America either (emigrated, immigrated) from another country or descended from someone who (emigrated, immigrated) to this one.

_____

_____

10. The kangaroo is one (kind of, kind of a) marsupial found only in Australia.

_____

_____

20.2 The Dictionary and Usage

■ *Look up each word in parentheses in a current dictionary to determine the correct choice. Underline the answer and write a summary of the usage rule under each sentence.*

1. (Fewer, Less) than half of the presidents of the United States were born outside the original thirteen colonies.

_____

_____

_____

2. Unshaven and red-eyed, the newspaper editor looked (as if, like) he had worked for days without sleep.

_____

_____

_____

3. Smiling broadly, the captain of the debate team (accepted, excepted) the trophy.

_____

_____

_____

4. Can anyone tell (who's, whose) signature this is?

_____

_____

_____

5. When we came (inside, inside of) the arena, we were deafened by the roar of the crowd.

_____

_____

_____

6. The back porch was (partly, partially) shaded from the morning sun by tall pines to the east.

_____

_____

_____

7. For the coffee merchant, inhaling the aroma of the roasting Colombian beans was a (sensuous, sensual) pleasure.

_____

_____

_____

8. Conscientious campers (try to, try and) find safe, wind-free places to build cooking fires.

_____

_____

_____

9. Alarmed by strong currents and rising wind, the skipper called for a weather report before deciding whether or not to (precede, proceed) with the cruise.

_____

_____

_____

10. (These Kinds, These kind) of foods are high in fat: butter, cream, bacon, and avocado.

_____

_____

_____

20.3 The Dictionary and Usage

■ *Look up each word in parentheses in a current dictionary to determine the correct choice. Underline the answer and write a summary of the usage rule under each sentence.*

1. For many Americans, reading the newspaper is an (everyday, every day) occurrence.

   _____

   _____

   _____

2. After graduation, well-prepared chemical engineers can expect to find a job that pays (good, well).

   _____

   _____

   _____

3. Bankers agreed that the very slight increase in inflation would have little (affect, effect) on interest rates.

   _____

   _____

   _____

4. The candidate politely begged to (differ from, differ with) his distinguished colleague.

   _____

   _____

   _____

5. I was surprised to learn that the temperature of an oven drops about twenty-five degrees (every, ever) time the door is opened.

_____

_____

_____

6. The hot, thirsty campers saw the glimmer of a waterfall a long (way, ways) off.

_____

_____

_____

7. Although she was trained in cellular biology, the graduate student found it difficult to distinguish (among, between) three species of bacteria.

_____

_____

_____

8. After studying for (awhile, a while), the students ordered a pizza.

_____

_____

_____

9. When we saw the Secret Service agents step forward, we knew that the president's arrival was (eminent, imminent).

_____

_____

_____

10. Teasing (each other, one another) mercilessly, the basketball players returned to the locker room after a long practice.

_____

_____

_____

20.4 The Dictionary and Usage

■ *Look up each word in parentheses in a current dictionary to determine the correct choice. Underline the answer and write a summary of the usage rule under each sentence.*

1. After a local referendum the dome of the (capital, capitol) building was cleaned and repaired.

   _____

   _____

   _____

2. Doris Lessing, a British writer, has written (many, a lot of) novels, including science fiction and horror novels.

   _____

   _____

   _____

3. The traffic officer signaled that it was (alright, all right) for us to drive through the intersection.

   _____

   _____

   _____

4. Because of a shortage of bamboo shoots, (fewer, less) pandas than expected will survive a severe winter.

   _____

   _____

   _____

5. Thousands of young fans waited (anxiously, eagerly) for the concert to begin.

_____

_____

_____

6. The instructor showed his class a video that (complemented, complimented) his lecture on the Komodo dragon.

_____

_____

_____

7. Management eventually (agreed to, agreed with) almost all of the union's demands.

_____

_____

_____

8. The (continual, continuous) regimen of daily exercise, fresh air, and healthy food soon improved his spirits.

_____

_____

_____

9. Finding a parking space is an (everyday, every day) problem for commuters who work downtown.

_____

_____

_____

10. The police officer stopped the oncoming motorist, who had already driven a long (way, ways) with only his parking lights on.

_____

_____

_____

20.5 The Dictionary and Usage

■ *Underline each example of poor usage and write the correction underneath each sentence. No sentence contains more than two such examples. One sentence is correct.*

EXAMPLE

The executive complained that the attempt to <u>finalize</u> <u>those sort</u> of deals was frustrating.

_____ *formalize; those sorts* _____

1. After catching the bus into the city, we spent a while in the museum, then enjoyed a quite Italian dinner.

   _____

2. Over two million boys in America are effected by hyperactivity, a disorder that some believe contributes later to alcoholism.

   _____

3. We received a letter from the bursary in regards to a late registration fee.

   _____

4. The reason the barbershop quartet performed so many nostalgic numbers is because the audience requested those sort.

   _____

5. Seeing the sun rise over the Great Pyramids is the kind of a memory the world traveler will cherish for a lifetime.

   _____

6. The Ferris wheel whirled all together too fast like it were about to spin away into the sky.

   _____

7. Most of the refugees who emigrate to the United States eventually find productive and satisfying jobs.

   _____

8. Fewer than half of the people who attended the opening night of *Aïda* wore formal dress; consequently, sequined dresses appeared besides jeans.

_____

9. Christmas is a time when many families gather to exchange gifts and to visit with one another.

_____

10. Some cooks put oregano, paprika, and sage in to their chili.

_____

20.6 The Dictionary and Usage

■ *Underline each example of poor usage and write the correction underneath each sentence. No sentence contains more than two such examples.*

1. The average American grocery store is much larger today than in the 1970s, including more then twice as many square feet and up to five times as many items.

   _____

2. A large amount of people worked on the Erie Canal.

   _____

3. Tom stood in the lobby for almost an hour before he left, tired of waiting on his group members to arrive.

   _____

4. Curling, a winter sport which dates from the 1500s, first appeared as a gold-medal competition in the 1998 Olympics.

   _____

5. A brownout is when lights are partially dimmed or extinguished because of a power reduction.

   _____

6. When in New York City, try and see the Statue of Liberty and the Empire State Building.

   _____

7. The committee members were already to elect a new chair until they realized that they lacked a quorum.

   _____

8. The main reason why Marvin disliked his job was because it offered him few opportunities for advancement.

   _____

9. For the new high school, the school board selected a principle with many years of teaching experience.

_____

10. Phototropism is where plants turn toward their source of light.

_____

NAME _____

DATE _____ SCORE _____

20.7 The Dictionary and Usage: Review 1

■ *Underline each example of poor usage and write the corrections above each line.*

For thousands of years, societies around the world spent alot of time try-

ing to devise an accurate calendar. Many early calendars were based on the

lunar cycle rather than the solar cycle. However, since lunar months are less

then thirty days long, a lunar year is only 354 days. Early astronomers

learned that lunar calendars could still conform with the solar year, provided

they added seven extra months over the course of nineteen years. Other an-

cient astronomers based their calendars on a different principal, the length

of time it takes the sun to return to the exact position in the sky. As early as

7,000 years ago, Egyptians were using the sun to create a 365-day calendar

that was distinctly different than the lunar calendars used throughout the

Mediterranean region. Remarkably, by noting the annual alignment of the

sun to the star we call Sirius, they came to realize that the solar year is ac-

tually some six hours longer than 365 days. The ancient Maya and Aztec

peoples also had 365-day calendars to structure there years, and the archi-

tects of Stonehenge could measure within minutes the true time our planet

takes to revolve around the sun.

Adapted from David Ewing Duncan, "Calendar,"
Smithsonian 29, no. 11 (1999): 48–58.

20.8 The Dictionary and Usage: Review 2

■ *Underline each example of poor usage and write the corrections above each line.*

A large amount of people would agree to the idea that going to the cir-

cus was an exciting childhood event. The atmosphere itself had a special

tang; even the sawdust hanging in the air was a sensual pleasure as if, for

awhile, one could both smell and taste the excitement. What a thrill it was

when the lights dimmed and the trapeze artist flew over the crowds like a

bird on the wing, and how the audience jumped when the clown suddenly

bursted a balloon filled with water! Surely nothing can compare to the heart-

stopping experience of seeing the unprotected lion tamer taunting the king

of the beasts, who, snarling and growling, was ready to hurl himself off of

the ledge in his cage. Irregardless of the time, the end always came too

quickly; parents were already to leave while children still sat starry-eyed,

clutching the remains of sticky candied apples or crumpled bags of popcorn.

20.9 The Dictionary and Standard English

■ *With the aid of a dictionary, label the italicized words as* **formal, informal, colloquial,** *and so on. Replace nonstandard expressions with equivalents in Standard English.*

EXAMPLE

The mechanic said he was *fixing to* begin work on my car.   *regional;*
about

1. Many prospectors passed *thru* British Columbia on their way to the Yukon during the famous Klondike gold rush.   _____

2. Before contracting with a personal trainer, be sure he is someone you can *count on* to provide an individualized fitness program.   _____

3. We found it *plenty* easy to earn extra income by selling scrap aluminum.   _____

4. In *A Clockwork Orange,* Anthony Burgess describes a London terrorized by a *bunch of punks.*   _____

5. Alexander Graham Bell was issued a patent for his most famous invention, the *phone,* on March 7, 1886.   _____

6. The avid collectors continued to bid on the antique car, *irregardless* of its cost.   _____

7. Many listeners were extremely *mad* when they learned that Orson Welles's *War of the Worlds* was fiction, not fact.   _____

8. We felt *gypped* when the concert was canceled and the promoters refused to refund our tickets.   _____

9. Recently referees have begun to penalize players for *talking trash.*   _____

10. A good health care plan will not require either physicians or hospitals to *cut corners.*   _____

20.10 The Dictionary and Standard English

■ *For each of the following, supply an appropriate expression in Standard English.*

EXAMPLE

flaky _____ *not dependable* _____

1. double-cross _____

2. anyways _____

3. lousy _____

4. plain as day _____

5. enthused _____

6. lots of _____

7. nosy _____

8. hook, line, and sinker _____

9. chummy _____

10. goes to show _____

11. hock _____

12. tote _____

13. can't hardly _____

14. would not of _____

15. couple of _____

16. spooky _____

17. could of _____

18. sort of _____

19. being as _____

20. must of _____

20.11 Improprieties

■ *Circle the improprieties in the following phrases and correct them in the blanks at the right. If you find none, write* **C** *in the blank.*

EXAMPLE

(occupation) hazards _____ *occupational* _____

1. reforming institution policies _____

2. to be taken for granite _____

3. a careful developed plan _____

4. respectively yours _____

5. a stationery object _____

6. a poor paid employee _____

7. a wood baseball bat _____

8. a considerable harder problem _____

9. a commanding presents _____

10. a thin-skin person _____

11. a careful designed study _____

12. a quiet convincing argument _____

13. an unequip ship _____

14. a clearly executed plan _____

15. a resonance voice _____

16. the spokened word _____

17. the rein of Louis XIV _____

18. a handwriting letter _____

19. a waterlog field _____

20. a meander stream _____

21. dry, sand soil _____

22. to make an enlighten comment _____

23. a monster wave _____

24. mystery phenomena _____

25. ivy tendoned to the walls _____

20.12 Improprieties

■ *Choose the correct word and write it in the blank at the right. Consult a dictionary if necessary.*

EXAMPLE
Only (two, to, too) species of the cat family are presently facing possible extinction in India—the Asian lion and the Bengal tiger.

two

1. No one is sure exactly (were, where) Columbus and his crew first set foot in the New World.

_____

2. The physics exam was (too, two, to) difficult.

_____

3. One anti-drug-abuse campaign was led by a (formal, former) Miss America.

_____

4. Dozens of legislators gathered on the steps of the (capital, capitol) for their annual photograph.

_____

5. Money was available to (aid, aide) the victims of the flood.

_____

6. All of the participants in the marriage workshop reported an improvement in their (marital, martial) relationships.

_____

7. The school board voted to (raise, raze) the old gymnasium and build a new sports complex.

_____

8. The governor decided to stand by her (principles, principals) and vote against the bill.

_____

9. Some amusement parks employ workers to provide (assistance, assistants) to visitors.

_____

10. *Dances with Wolves* is an (epoch, epic) film about the American West.

_____

11. Fried fish and (cole, cold, coal) slaw are a favorite culinary combination.

_____

12. Among other things, guidance (councilors, coun-selors) help students schedule classes and apply to colleges.

_____

13. Young male drivers pay higher insurance rates be-cause statistically (there, they're, their) more likely to have an accident.

_____

14. Every winter, millions of Americans fantasize about vacationing on an (aisle, isle) in the South Pacific.

_____

15. Setting a new record at the marathon was a great (fete, feat) for the runner.

_____

16. Only a few students caught the professor's passing (allusion, illusion) to Norse mythology.

_____

17. (Passed, Past) over by all the political pundits, the dark-horse candidate emerged the winner of the state primary.

_____

18. (Preceding, Proceeding) along migratory routes, wild geese often fly in easily recognizable formations.

_____

19. Physicians (prescribe, proscribe) antibiotics for most respiratory infections.

_____

20. After running up three flights of stairs, I was out of (breath, breathe) and weak-kneed.

_____

21. The anthropologist had spent five years studying the fertility (rights, rites) of three small tribes living in the Amazon basin.

_____

22. The general (moral, morale) of the nation usually in-creases after a presidential election.

_____

23. The space shuttle can release (it's, its) payload while deep in space.

_____

24. The city was (greatful, grateful) for the contributions to the library fund.

_____

25. With his exploits celebrated in more than sixty lan-guages, Arthur Conan Doyle's Sherlock Holmes (maybe, may be) the most popular detective ever portrayed in fiction.

_____

20.13 Improprieties and Usage

■ *Underline each impropriety or usage error. Write the corrections above each line.*

Sometimes called *caribe* or *capaburro,* the piranha has illicited fear

among Americans ever sense Teddy Roosevelt called it "the most dangerous

fish in the world." In its natural habitat, however, this creature only occa-

sionally lives up to it's fearsome reputation. According to one study, too of

the three most common kinds of piranha survive by nipping the scales and

fins of other fish. For this reason, some researchers consider them parasites

rather then predators. Others feed primarily on nuts and seeds. The red-

bellied piranha, though, does regularly feed on flesh. Where their are large

concentrations, for example, along river banks where fishermen clean their

catch, these piranha can and do live up to there reputation, skeletonizing

carcasses in a matter of minutes or even seconds. Under more typical con-

ditions, villagers wade passed groups of red-bellied piranha without fear.

Such facts have little affect on this fish's reputation as a vicious killer. Al-

though not completely fare, its bad reputation will last as long as these tooth-

some denizens of the Amazon basin continue to live.

Adapted from Richard Coniff, "Relax, It's Only a Piranha,"
Smithsonian 30, no. 4 (1999): 42–50.

20.14 Homonyms and Improprieties

Homonyms are words that sound alike but differ in both spelling and meaning. The use of the incorrect homonym leads to an impropriety.

EXAMPLES

bore: to drill   *peace:* freedom from war   *lesson:* instruction

boar: male pig   *piece:* part of a whole   *lessen:* to reduce

■ *Write the correct homonym in the blank.*

EXAMPLE

For the document to become official, the (ceil, seal) of a notary public is required.   *seal*

1. The Space Age has seen the proliferation of an astonishing array of (new, knew) technologies.   _____

2. A golfer's dream is to get a (hole-, whole-) in-one.   _____

3. The students complained that the grammar exercise was (to, two, too) difficult.   _____

4. Valentine's Day revolves around the tradition of giving (presents, presence) to the one you love.   _____

5. In the new business venture, Diane's outgoing personality was an effective (compliment, complement) to Harry's more reserved nature.   _____

6. During the Great Depression, some former landowners found it necessary to (pedal, peddle) produce from door to door.   _____

7. In Ursula K. Le Guin's *The Left Hand of Darkness*, (there, they're, their) exists a world where humans are both male and female.   _____

8. Aaron Burr, vice president of the United States from 1801 to 1805, killed Alexander Hamilton in a (dual, duel) in 1804.   _____

9. Many new cars have sophisticated antilock (brake, break) systems.   _____

10. Many people do not (no, know) that Earth has two north poles: true north and magnetic north. _____

11. In the Middle Ages, the (bore, boar) was often regarded as a symbol of courage and strength. _____

12. "(Eye, eye; Aye, aye), Captain," said the sailor. _____

13. Charlotte's favorite saddle horse has a really smooth (gate, gait). _____

14. Fishing conditions frequently (very, vary) with water temperatures. _____

15. The expedition members readied themselves for the short (assent, ascent) to the mesa summit. _____

16. The nursing student had some trouble locating the patient's (vain, vane, vein). _____

17. The journalist (sighted, sited, cited) anonymous sources in her article on political corruption. _____

18. Aztec priests regularly offered human sacrifices on sacred (alters, altars). _____

19. Margaret found her great-grandmother's wedding (vale, veil) in a trunk in the attic. _____

20. My curiosity was (peaked, piqued) by the sound of someone playing a steel guitar. _____

20.15 Idioms

■ *Circle faulty idioms in the following sentences. Write correct idioms in the blanks at the right.*

EXAMPLE
Your house looks very similar (with) ours.   _____*to*_____

1. In the year of 1922, T. S. Eliot published one of the most influential poems of the century.   _____

2. Many people around the world still die from inadequate sanitation and poor nutrition.   _____

3. The second version of the popular spreadsheet program was almost identical from the first.   _____

4. Many teachers find that attractive classrooms are conducive of learning.   _____

5. The puma and the wolf were once indigenous of almost every state in the union.   _____

6. Concerned about his grades, Jeremy did not wait on his instructor to return the latest test but instead made an appointment to see a tutor immediately.   _____

7. Be sure and proofread your research paper for spelling errors.   _____

8. Although Ponce de Leon spent a lot of time and money searching on the Fountain of Youth, he was never convinced that it really existed.   _____

9. My father planned on visiting some relatives in Dallas over the Christmas holidays.   _____

10. Gazpacho is a type of a cold soup that is very popular in Spain.   _____

20.16 Triteness

■ *Revise the following sentences to eliminate triteness.*

EXAMPLE
I decided to take the bull by the horns.

I decided to confront the problem.
_____

1. In today's complex society, students need to develop their problem-solving skills.

   _____

   _____

   _____

2. She was a fair-weather friend who was never around in the clinches.

   _____

   _____

   _____

3. Enlistment in the military grew by leaps and bounds during the first few weeks of World War II.

   _____

   _____

   _____

4. "You have bought during a declining market," said the doleful stockbroker to her disheartened client, "but if at first you don't succeed, try, try again."

   _____

   _____

   _____

5. San Francisco, a city that has twice rebuilt after suffering the effects of devastating earthquakes, is proof that every cloud has a silver lining.

_____

_____

_____

6. Each and every one of my tried and true classmates told me straight from the shoulder that she would write to me at college.

_____

_____

_____

7. In this day and age, people from all walks of life use computers each and every day.

_____

_____

_____

8. Medical students with liberal arts degrees are few and far between.

_____

_____

_____

9. In the final analysis, an ounce of prevention is worth a pound of cure.

_____

_____

_____

10. Good accounts are worth their weight in gold in the current business climate.

_____

_____

_____

20.17 Triteness

■ *Underline the clichés and trite phrases appearing in the following paragraph. Then rephrase the passage using fresher language.*

It is no deep, dark secret that the Persian Wars of ancient Greece altered forever the shape of Mediterranean civilization. When King Darius of Persia sent a force to the Greek coast in 490 B.C., he thought victory had been sewn up. However, a much smaller but determined force from the city of Athens responded as quick as lightning, defeated the invaders at the Battle of Marathon, and in doing so preserved the democratic government that city had instituted only eighteen years earlier. However, the Persians were not content to live and let live, and King Darius's son, Xerxes, returned with an even greater force in 479 B.C. Once again, the Greeks put their shoulders to the wheel and came through in a pinch. Deciding this time that wisdom was the better part of valor, the Athenians abandoned their city, let the Persians destroy it, then lured the Persian navy into the straits of Salamis. Here a fleet of Greek triremes surprised their enemy, sank hundreds of ships, and forced Xerxes and his forces to return to Persia with their tails between their legs. Once again, the fledgling democracy survived. If not for these two victories, the political evolution of Western Europe might have been very different.

21 Wordiness and Repetition

WORDINESS

- Avoid using many words when one or two will serve.

NOT

The envelope containing the electric bill was delivered today. [nine words]

BUT

The electric bill came today. [five words]

- Avoid overuse of the passive voice (in which the subject is acted upon).

NOT

My new W-2 form was mailed to me by my employer. [eleven words]

BUT

My employer mailed me my new W-2 form. [eight words]

- Revise long sentences to achieve concision.

NOT

I wish to say that I have not at this moment fully engaged in this warlike action. [seventeen words]

BUT

I have not yet begun to fight. [seven words]

- Avoid dependence on *it is, there is,* and *there are.*

NOT

It is essential for the house to be painted.

BUT

The house must be painted.

NOT

There are only two application forms left.

BUT

Only two application forms are left.

REPETITION

Avoid excessive repetition of words, synonyms, and sounds.

NOT

The book on the table is a book about buccaneers in the South Seas.

BUT

The book on the table is about buccaneers in the South Seas.

NOT

The wind sifted sparks from the sizzling blaze.

BUT

The wind blew sparks from the blaze.

21.1 Wordiness

■ *Revise the following sentences to make them concise.*

EXAMPLE
Alison spoke in a forceful manner.

_____ *Alison spoke forcefully.* _____

1. It was William Harvey who first wrote about the circulation of the blood.

   _____

   _____

2. In terms of the size of its land, Canada is the second-largest country in the world.

   _____

   _____

3. The movie *Gone with the Wind* is a film that is based on a novel by Margaret Mitchell.

   _____

   _____

4. After the Battle of Waterloo, Napoleon was exiled to the island of St. Helena by the British.

   _____

   _____

5. Simón Bolívar is considered by many people to be a hero because of his work in helping defeat, through armed conflict, the Spanish armies in South America.

   _____

   _____

6. The number of white rhinos was affected by hunting in such a way that the number of rhinos declined in number from four hundred to fewer than twenty during the fifteen years between 1970 and 1985.

_____

_____

7. It has been shown that the duration of the common cold can be reduced by giving the person with the cold doses of zinc glutonate in the form of lozenges.

_____

_____

8. In the times in which we live, people just can hardly be independent any longer. Look what is happening to them in the field of education. They cannot think for themselves. This is also true in other areas of life.

_____

_____

9. Many municipalities have begun recycling programs due to the fact that their landfills are filling up with waste.

_____

_____

10. After reviewing the evidence in your case that was presented by your lawyer to me, we realize that there is some justification and warrant for a new trial.

_____

_____

21.2 Wordiness

■ *Revise the following sentences to make them concise.*

EXAMPLE

I went to the theater for the reason that I wanted to see the first film by Alfred Hitchcock.

I went to the theater to see Alfred Hitchcock's first film.

1. There is a real resistance to corporal punishment on the part of many child psychologists.

    _____

    _____

2. Tchaikovsky's three ballets—*Swan Lake, Sleeping Beauty,* and *The Nutcracker*—are ballets that are so very popular today for the reason that they make classical ballet accessible to the modern audience.

    _____

    _____

3. In his day and time and in the community that he lived in, Henry David Thoreau was considered to be eccentric by his neighbors.

    _____

    _____

4. Most eye-catching advertisements in magazines attract the reader's attention with designs that are bold and colors that are bright.

    _____

    _____

5. An ovenbird is an American bird that is a member of the warbler family and that builds a nest that resembles an oven on the floor of a forest.

_____

_____

6. Traditional zoos are considered by most authorities to be detrimental to animals due to the fact that they deny animals truly natural conditions in which they can live.

_____

_____

7. For years and years the basic cultural foundation of this great nation was the small town with its small, homogeneous neighborhoods and communal cohesion.

_____

_____

8. Beginning in the 1930s and continuing through several decades down to the present time, writers have often been interested in Hollywood as a setting for their novels.

_____

_____

9. There are usually research assistants at major universities to help and assist professors to do a large number of research projects.

_____

_____

10. Old-growth forests are forests that are at least two hundred years old and that have never been cut.

_____

_____

21.3 Repetition

■ *Revise the following sentences to eliminate ineffective repetition.*

EXAMPLE
All of the indicators indicate that the show will be a success.

All of the indicators suggest that the show will be a success.

1. Instant replays show that officials usually make correct calls and perform their duties both correctly and responsibly.

_____

_____

2. The story of Hansel and Gretel reflects children's fear of being left alone or abandoned and having to become independent and to care for themselves.

_____

_____

3. Both of the halfbacks were both agile and powerful runners.

_____

_____

4. Most large cities are circumscribed by large beltways that help to decrease large traffic jams.

_____

_____

5. The cuisine of the Mediterranean features a varied mixture of different kinds of foods, including foods from southern Europe and the Islamic world.

_____

_____

6. Advertisers who want to advertise their products on the radio use catchy slogans and memorable phrases to appeal to listeners.

_____

_____

7. Sewing one's own clothes is a way of saving money and allows one to choose one's favorite style and one's favorite fabric.

_____

_____

8. Successful football teams that win often have kickers who kick field goals and kick extra points well.

_____

_____

9. House plants give a house a fresh and inviting appearance unless too many are crowded into a small house.

_____

_____

10. Of all the assessment measures used to assess students' academic abilities, aptitude tests and grade point averages are the most common.

_____

_____

21.4 Repetition

■ *Revise the following sentences to eliminate ineffective repetition.*

EXAMPLE
I propose that we further study this proposal.

____We need to study this proposal further.____

1. The heavy debts of many debt-ridden countries are straining the debt-carrying capacity of the international monetary community.

   _____

   _____

2. MTV is a television network on television that has changed the way producers and artists have marketed their products on the market.

   _____

   _____

3. A cup of raisins contains almost eight times as many calories as a cup of strawberries contains.

   _____

   _____

4. Farmers who farm the rich soil of the Midwest produce most of the wheat produced in this country.

   _____

   _____

5. Today's service-based economy offers many jobs in the service sector to those willing to serve the public.

   _____

   _____

6. The fashions designed by the major fashion designers are generally targeted at young, fashion-conscious consumers.

_____

_____

7. Innovative architects have begun to use solar energy to harness the sun's power to heat homes and even to generate electricity.

_____

_____

8. Sand painting, the ancient art of creating pictures with colored sand, was first originated by Native Americans for their ancient rituals.

_____

_____

9. Some elk from overpopulated elk herds in Yellowstone National Park have been exported to other parks in other regions and even to other countries.

_____

_____

10. Fiberglass insulation is frequently used to insulate both the walls and ceilings.

_____

_____

21.5 Wordiness and Repetition

■ *Revise the following paragraph to eliminate wordiness and unnecessary repetition.*

In terms of recovering in number, many endangered species are increasing dramatically because of protective measures. Perhaps the best-known species that was in danger of becoming extinct was the bald eagle, but today the species is reproducing nicely. It is widely known that creating a ban on the use of DDT was a great help in contributing to this recovery. In a similar way, there is a larger number of American alligators living now than there was only a few years ago. Because of a ban on hunting, alligators are not only thriving in Florida, where over a million live, but they are also found in a region stretching from the state of Oklahoma in the West to North Carolina in the East. During the decade of the 1920s, there were only approximately a half-million white-tailed deer. Today the population of this animal is over fourteen million. It is the opinion of most authorities that this increase is due to the fact that there is much more forest land in the eastern half of the United States than there was eighty years ago. Through the efforts of farmers and hunters, among other people, including environmentalists, the number of elk, moose, turkeys, geese, and black bears are on the upswing, too, in a manner of speaking.

Adapted from Robert Gordon Jr. and George Dunlop, "Creature Comfort:
The Revitalization of American Wildlife," *Policy Review* (Summer 1990).

22 Connotation, Figurative Language, Flowery Language, Sexist Language, and Vocabulary

CONNOTATION

Words often have special associations called connotations. **Denotations** of words are their precise meanings. Denotatively, the word *home* simply refers to a dwelling place. Connotatively, the word suggests several emotional reactions relating to family, friends, and special occasions.

Good writers attempt to find words that have the right associations, those that work most effectively.

EXAMPLE

Frances is *skinny.* [*Skinny* has a negative connotation.]
Frances is *slender.* [*Slender* has a positive connotation.]

FIGURATIVE LANGUAGE

Avoid mixed and inappropriate figures of speech. Mixed figures associate things that are not logically related.

EXAMPLE

As an administrator, her Achilles' heel was riding roughshod over the accounts department, which was only fishing in troubled waters.

IMPROVED

As an administrator, her weakness was dealing too harshly with the accounts department, which was in disarray.

Use figurative comparisons to create originality.

EXAMPLE

Language is the cornerstone of civilization. [metaphor]

Opportunity is *like* a good mystery story; you never know what will happen when you turn the page. [simile]

FLOWERY LANGUAGE

Avoid ornate or pretentious language. Make your sentences clear.

PLAIN LANGUAGE	FLOWERY LANGUAGE
here	in this world in which we live and work
pen	this writing instrument
finally	having reached the termination of this discourse

SEXIST LANGUAGE

Sexist language is language that assigns roles or characteristics to individuals on the basis of gender. Using only masculine nouns and pronouns to refer to both sexes is often considered sexist. To avoid sexist language, rephrase your sentences to eliminate generic masculine nouns and pronouns as labels based on gender. Below are some helpful rules to follow:

1. Avoid using *he, him* (masculine pronouns) when referring to both sexes.

NOT

A pilot is responsible for *his* passengers.

BUT

A pilot is responsible for *his* or *her* passengers.

PREFERRED

Pilots are responsible for *their* passengers. [Use plural.]

ALTERNATIVE

A pilot is responsible for *the passengers.* [Avoid using pronoun.]

2. Avoid using *man* to refer to both sexes.

NOT

Man is a rational animal.

BUT

People are rational animals.

NOT

Peace on earth; goodwill to *men.*

BUT

Peace on earth; goodwill to *all.*

NOT

Global warming affects *mankind.*

BUT

Global warming affects *humanity* (or *everyone*).

3. Avoid using sexist job titles.

NOT

The *chairman* of the department has to be an excellent *spokesman.*

BUT

The *chair* (or *chairperson*) of the department has to be an excellent *speaker* (or *spokesperson*).

22.1 Connotation

■ *Words that have approximately the same denotation frequently suggest meanings that are different. The combinations that follow bring together words with different connotations. In the spaces at the right, rate each word in terms of its favorability of connotation: 1 for most favorable, 2 for less favorable, and 3 for least favorable. Be prepared to defend your decisions and to explain the different shades of connotation.*

EXAMPLE

frugal	*2*
cheap	*3*
inexpensive	*1*

1. flashy	_____	6. devout	_____
bright	_____	pious	_____
gaudy	_____	saintly	_____
2. gaunt	_____	7. absurd	_____
thin	_____	silly	_____
slender	_____	preposterous	_____
3. run away	_____	8. conspicuous	_____
escape	_____	obtrusive	_____
desert	_____	obvious	_____
4. dislike	_____	9. abstemious	_____
disapprove	_____	self-controlled	_____
detest	_____	temperate	_____
5. exhausted	_____	10. pleasure	_____
worn out	_____	amusement	_____
tired	_____	titillation	_____

11. debate _____

    discuss _____

    argue _____

12. simple _____

    naive _____

    innocent _____

13. impulsive _____

    spontaneous _____

    unconstrained _____

14. famous _____

    notorious _____

    well-known _____

15. guess _____

    premonition _____

    hunch _____

16. bright _____

    brainy _____

    intelligent _____

17. beautiful _____

    cute _____

    pretty _____

18. smell _____

    stench _____

    odor _____

19. malleable _____

    tractable _____

    cooperative _____

20. speech _____

    tirade _____

    harangue _____

21. lie _____

    deception _____

    falsehood _____

22. visionary _____

    dreamer _____

    romantic _____

23. illegal _____

    unlawful _____

    criminal _____

24. rambling _____

    episodic _____

    digressive _____

25. request _____

    solicit _____

    beg _____

22.2 Connotation

■ *Words that have approximately the same denotation frequently suggest meanings that are different. The combinations that follow bring together words with different connotations. In the spaces at the right, rate each word in terms of its favorability of connotation:* 1 *for most favorable,* 2 *for less favorable, and* 3 *for least favorable. Be prepared to defend your decisions and to explain the different shades of connotation.*

EXAMPLE

rehearse   *1*

practice   *2*

drill   *3*

1. sketch	_____	6. cordial	_____
caricature	_____	friendly	_____
drawing	_____	sociable	_____
2. temperate	_____	7. intentions	_____
self-denying	_____	design	_____
austere	_____	end	_____
3. offensive	_____	8. determined	_____
repulsive	_____	stubborn	_____
revolting	_____	uncompromising	_____
4. thrifty	_____	9. motive	_____
stingy	_____	incentive	_____
parsimonious	_____	inducement	_____
5. employee	_____	10. abundant	_____
worker	_____	profuse	_____
laborer	_____	plentiful	_____

11. emotional   _____

    passionate   _____

    excitable   _____

12. eccentricity   _____

    foible   _____

    quirk   _____

13. different   _____

    abnormal   _____

    deviant   _____

14. plead   _____

    argue   _____

    exhort   _____

15. normal   _____

    mediocre   _____

    commonplace   _____

16. generous   _____

    lavish   _____

    extravagant   _____

17. distinguished _____

    noted   _____

    renowned   _____

18. wealthy   _____

    rich   _____

    opulent   _____

19. crowd   _____

    horde   _____

    throng   _____

20. habitual   _____

    customary   _____

    conventional   _____

21. healthy   _____

    robust   _____

    well   _____

22. choosy   _____

    selective   _____

    finicky   _____

23. guilty   _____

    delinquent   _____

    transgressive _____

24. perseverance   _____

    obstinacy   _____

    doggedness   _____

25. deteriorate   _____

    rot   _____

    decompose   _____

22.3 Figurative Language

■ *Here is a descriptive passage adapted from Eudora Welty's* Losing Battles. *Fill in the blanks, using the following list of Welty's images and figures of speech.*

pyramid	copper-colored	rocked into
tearing out	barking	caught up with
bumped across	packed	carried a cargo

A wall of [1] _____ dust came moving up the hill. It was

being brought by a ten-year-old Chevrolet sedan that had been made into a

hauler by [2] _____ the back seat and the window glass. It

[3] _____ the yard with a rider on the running board waving

in a pitcher's glove; [4] _____ inside with excited faces,

some dogs' faces among them, it [5] _____ of tomato bas-

kets spaced out on its roof, hood, and front fenders, every basket holding a

red and yellow [6] _____ of peaches. With the dogs in the

yard and the dogs in the car all [7] _____ together, the car

[8] _____ the yard to the pecan tree, halted behind the

school bus, and then the dust [9]_____ it.

22.4 Flowery Language

Flowery language is language that is ornate or pretentious. Avoid flowery language by writing in a clear and direct style.

■ *Revise the following sentences to eliminate flowery language.*

EXAMPLE
The inside of a geode glitters with the silvery radiance of sidereal splendor.

The inside of a geode sparkles with crystals.

1. We gazed lovingly at the puffy cotton balls in the clear blue sky.

   _____

   _____

2. As a young boy, I frequently stood rapt beneath the spangled vault of heaven, transfixed by the nocturnal cacophony of whippoorwills.

   _____

   _____

3. Many cardiologists advise a swift retreat from the ambrosial condiments of the evening repast.

   _____

   _____

4. The stirring harmonies and rousing melodic lines of John Philip Sousa's immortal march entitled "Stars and Stripes Forever" never fail to quicken my heart with patriotic fervor.

   _____

   _____

5. The young trick-or-treaters dressed as cadaverous denizens of Count Dracula's castle.

   _____

   _____

6. Two frolicsome kittens gamboled gaily among the blossoming stalks of springtime.

_____

_____

7. The venerable institution of holy matrimony has become the object of much sociological research in the hallowed halls of academia.

_____

_____

8. The drowsy fumes of Morpheus conquered us as the boring speaker droned in monotonous monotone.

_____

_____

9. Every New Year's Eve, we celebrate the fledgling moments of Earth's fresh diurnal round with a flavorful repast of wine, cheese, and chocolate.

_____

_____

10. The lofty reaches of the craggy tops of the mountains were covered by the freezing precipitation that fell in a frenzied swirl.

_____

_____

22.5 Vocabulary

■ *In the blank at the right, place the letter of the word or phrase you believe is nearest in meaning to the italicized word. You may guess; then consult a dictionary.*

EXAMPLE

sumptuous meals: (a) delicious, (b) carefully prepared, (c) lavish

_____ *c* _____

1. a *defunct* issue: (a) overdrawn, (b) boring, (c) dead

_____

2. a *heinous* act: (a) kind, (b) reprehensible, (c) outrageous

_____

3. a *cogent* argument: (a) clear, (b) concise, (c) convincing

_____

4. a *vitriolic* comment: (a) blunt, (b) baffling, (c) bitter

_____

5. an *obdurate* opponent: (a) unyielding, (b) timid, (c) clever

_____

6. to *aver* her innocence: (a) to declare, (b) to hint, (c) to believe

_____

7. *gauche* behavior: (a) suave, (b) awkward, (c) funny

_____

8. a *gratuitous* insult: (a) unwarranted, (b) deserved, (c) vehement

_____

9. to *foist* an idea: (a) to explain, (b) to develop (c) to impose

_____

10. a *verbose* lecturer: (a) dynamic, (b) wordy, (c) boring

_____

11. please *elucidate:* (a) explain, (b) denounce, (c) arrange

_____

12. *peremptory* treatment: (a) sensitive, (b) overbearing, (c) careful

_____

13. a *palpable* untruth: (a) obvious, (b) insignificant, (c) possible   _____

14. to *opt* for freedom: (a) decide, (b) flee, (c) sing   _____

15. a *disparate* group of people: (a) essentially different, (b) dangerous, (c) capable of murder   _____

16. a *proletarian:* (a) wage earner, (b) revolutionary, (c) democrat   _____

17. to *disconcert* an audience: (a) entertain, (b) upset, (c) amaze   _____

18. an *austere* lifestyle: (a) generous, (b) luxuriant, (c) strict   _____

19. a *splenetic* personality: (a) lively, (b) forceful, (c) irritable   _____

20. an *irrevocable* decision: (a) irresponsible, (b) irreversible, (c) irrelevant   _____

22.6 Vocabulary

■ *In the blank at the right, place the letter of the word or phrase you believe is nearest in meaning to the italicized word. You may guess; then consult a dictionary.*

EXAMPLE

a *repugnant* appearance: (a) colorful, (b) tasteless, (c) repulsive _____*c*_____

1. a *salutary* effect: (a) impractical, (b) remedial, (c) stimulating _____

2. *desultory* talk: (a) insulting, (b) boring, (c) random _____

3. a *fecund* imagination: (a) fruitful, (b) fallow, (c) flimsy _____

4. an *overt* act: (a) subversive, (b) hostile, (c) open to view _____

5. to live in *ignominy:* (a) disgrace, (b) squalor, (c) ignorance _____

6. a *tenacious* defender: (a) puny, (b) hostile, (c) determined _____

7. a *tenuous* connection: (a) strong, (b) laughable, (c) weak _____

8. a *facetious* remark: (a) obvious, (b) witty, (c) angry _____

9. an *adventitious* meeting: (a) secretive, (b) accidental, (c) awkward _____

10. the *acrimonious* controversy: (a) bitter, (b) marital, (c) religious _____

11. a state of *desuetude:* (a) disuse, (b) disrepair, (c) detestation _____

12. a *trenchant* remark: (a) foolish, (b) biting, (c) appropriate _____

13. an *abstruse* formula: (a) difficult, (b) simple, (c) straightforward _____

14. the *epitome* of selfishness: (a) certitude, (b) antithesis, (c) embodiment _____

15. to *cajole* someone: (a) criticize, (b) coax, (c) pester _____

16. to *foment* revolution: (a) quell, (b) expose, (c) instigate _____

17. *fastidiously* dressed: (a) carefully, (b) prudishly, (c) stylishly _____

18. childish *prattle:* (a) chatter, (b) petulance, (c) mischief _____

19. to *refute* an argument: (a) summarize, (b) disprove, (c) begin _____

20. to treat with *levity:* (a) gaiety, (b) seriousness, (c) haste _____

NAME _____

DATE _____ SCORE _____

22.7 Avoiding Sexist Language

■ *Revise the following paragraph to eliminate sexist language.*

The average man on the street knows Hedy Lamarr only as a glamour girl of the 1930s and 1940s, but her life off-stage was as incredible as any Hollywood script. At age seventeen, the young Austrian beauty scandalized Europe by being the first member of the fairer sex to appear nude in a major motion picture. Two years later, she married a rich arms manufacturer who sold weapons to Nazi Germany and Fascist Italy. At their home, which later appeared as the castle in *The Sound of Music,* she entertained Hitler and Mussolini as well as hundreds of arms dealers. Coming to detest her husband and his associates, the entertainer escaped to England, then came to America. Here she contributed to the war effort in surprising ways. In one night, the brunette bombshell sold seven million dollars worth of war bonds by promising to kiss every man who bought at least $25,000 worth of bonds. She also had an idea for controlling torpedoes with radio waves. Changing the frequency of the waves in an apparently random way would mean no man could jam the transmission. Together with composer George Antheil, she was awarded patent 2,292,387 for a "Secret Communication System," which the two donated to the federal government as a part of their contribution to the war effort. Although their idea remained unused during World War II, it was employed during the Cuban missile crisis. Later, men used the same concept, known as *spread spectrum communications,* in cellular telephones, wireless computer connections, and other applications.

22.8 Nonsexist Job Titles

■ *Job titles that assume the sex of the worker are not acceptable. Find alternative titles for the following sexist job titles and write them in the spaces provided. If any titles are acceptable, write* C.

EXAMPLES

chair, chairperson

chairman

foreman   *supervisor*

attorney   *C*

waitress   *food server*

1. mailman _____

2. authoress _____

3. secretary _____

4. congressman _____

5. milkman _____

6. poetess _____

7. fireman _____

8. businessman _____

9. watchman _____

10. stewardess _____

11. mechanic _____

12. housewife _____

13. craftsman _____

14. landlord _____

15. sportsman _____

16. spokesman   _____

17. laborer   _____

18. surgeon   _____

19. papergirl   _____

20. anchorman   _____

21. statesman   _____

22. garbageman   _____

23. professor   _____

24. male nurse   _____

25. bank teller   _____

Paragraphs

23 Identifying Paragraphs and Sentence Functions

Paragraphs, like sentences, are distinct units of meaning. Although some paragraphs serve to introduce, to conclude, or to provide transitions, most are used to present and develop ideas. To be effective, each of these paragraphs must possess a single central idea, usually expressed in a **topic sentence.** In most paragraphs, the first sentence is the topic sentence. Notice how the first sentence of the following paragraph controls its direction and development.

> *In panda reproduction the incredible becomes common.* The gestation period is variable, 97 days to 163 days. Most births occur in late August or September. Newborns are about six inches long, and weigh a mere three to four ounces— or 1/900 the weight of the mother; their skin is pink and almost naked, and their eyes are sealed until they are more than a month old. They look like ill-designed rubber toys. Such an underdeveloped infant should need a gestation period of only 45 days. It appears that the panda has delayed implantation, a condition in which the fertilized egg divides a few times to the blastocyst stage and then floats free in the uterus for one and a half to four months before implanting and continuing its growth.
>
> George B. Schaller, "Secrets of the Wild Panda,"
> *National Geographic,* March 1986: 292.

As a general rule, the appearance of a topic sentence signals the beginning of a new paragraph.

Furthermore, every sentence within a paragraph should develop the topic sentence. Sentences that do not clearly support the point of the paragraph but are only vaguely related to its general subject are said to be digressive. In the paragraph below, the fourth sentence shifts in focus from the impact of new products on the soft-drink industry to their impact on consumers.

> The soft-drink business is in transition. Recent introductions of non-caffeine colas and of new artificial sweeteners for diet drinks have created new markets. Soft-drink producers who ignore these trends will soon face lower profits. *Some consumers are baffled by the wide range of choices in retail outlets.* Research indicates that these new markets are likely to grow well into the next decade.

Finally, every sentence in a well-focused paragraph must clearly fulfill an identifiable function. In addition to topic sentences, most paragraphs also contain phrases or sentences that help narrow the central idea. These are called **restrictive** elements. Although most paragraphs have a single restriction, more complex ones may have two or more. Most sentences in most paragraphs, though, offer **support** in the form of examples, facts, explanations, definitions, descriptions, or evidence. The sentences in most explanatory paragraphs follow the order of *topic—restriction—support.* Note that the following paragraphs, topic sentences are introduced with (T), restriction sentences and phrases with (R), and support sentences with (S).

(T) Most farmers don't get subsidies. (R) Participation in the basic crop-subsidy programs is voluntary, and most farmers stay away. (S) A study released in 1984 by the Senate Budget Committee found that the major subsidy programs covered only 21 percent of farms and 16.5 percent of farm acreage.

Gregg Easterbrook, "Making Sense of Agriculture,"
The Atlantic, July 1985: 63.

(T) Professional boxing is too brutal a sport for any civilized people to tolerate. (R) In the ring, (S) boxers routinely treat spectators to the sight of bruised skin, bloodied noses, torn lips, and swollen eyes. (S) Ray "Boom Boom" Mancini even treated viewers to the death of his opponent. (R) But the damage boxers inflict upon each other is not limited to injuries evident in the ring. (S) Sugar Ray Leonard had his career shortened by a torn retina in his right eye. (S) Muhammad Ali is now suffering from a form of Parkinson's disease caused, many doctors believe, by too many blows to the head.[1]

---

1. The division of paragraphs into topic, restriction, and illustration slots from A. L. Becker, "A Tagmemic Approach to Paragraph Analysis," reprinted in The Sentence and the Paragraph (Urbana, IL: National Council of Teachers of English, 1966), 33–38.

23.1 Paragraph Division

■ *Divide the following passage into paragraphs by inserting the sign ¶. The original passage contains three paragraphs.*

The Civil War is, for the American imagination, the great single event of our history. Without too much wrenching, it may, in fact, be said to *be* American history. Before the Civil War we had no history in the deepest and most inward sense. There was, of course, the noble vision of the Founding Fathers articulated in the Declaration and the Constitution—the dream of freedom incarnated in a more perfect union. But the Revolution did not create a nation except on paper; and too often in the following years the vision of the Founding Fathers, which men had suffered and died to validate, became merely a daydream of easy and automatic victories, a vulgar delusion of manifest destiny, a conviction of being a people divinely chosen to live on milk and honey at small expense. The vision had not been finally submitted to the test of history. There was little awareness of the cost of having a history. The anguished scrutiny of the meaning of the vision in experience had not become a national reality. It became a reality, and we became a nation, only with the Civil War. The Civil War is our only "felt" history—history lived in the national imagination. This is not to say that the War is always, and by all men, felt in the same way. Quite the contrary. But this fact is an index to the very complexity, depth, and fundamental significance of the event. It is an overwhelming and vital image of human, and national, experience.

Robert Penn Warren, *The Legacy of the Civil War.*
(Cambridge: Harvard University Press, 1961), 3–4.

23.2 Paragraph Division

■ *Divide the following passage into paragraphs by inserting the sign ¶. The original passage contains three paragraphs.*

The Internet is one of those subjects that make normally sensible people go squishy in the brain. Witness the debate over Internet taxes. We're told not to tax the Internet, and we're not supposed to wonder why. It's obvious. The Internet is the future. Don't kill it with taxes. This skillfully sidesteps the basic question: Why shouldn't the Internet be taxed like everything else? The answer is that it should. Exempting e-commerce (items sold over the Internet) from sales taxes makes no sense. It's a disguised subsidy that favors one type of business over another and could make tax avoidance a permanent feature of the Internet society. Ideally, the Internet ought to compete with traditional stores on an equal footing. People would buy online if e-commerce offered lower prices, more choices or greater convenience. They would not buy simply to avoid taxes. We are now subsidizing the Internet in precisely this way. All but five states (Alaska, Delaware, Montana, New Hampshire, and Oregon) have sales taxes. The typical rate is 5 percent. States raise about a third of their revenues (roughly $156 billion in 1998) from sales taxes. Most, though not all, products sold over the Internet can escape sales taxes—a situation that only Congress can change. Some e-commerce depends on this hidden subsidy.

Robert J. Samuelson, "Why Not Tax the Internet?"
Newsweek, 6 March 2000: 49.

23.3 Paragraph Division

■ *Divide the following passage into paragraphs by inserting the sign ¶. The original passage contains two paragraphs.*

In France, where I currently reside, there are biscuits flavored with anisette and orange flower water and, of course, the traditional meringues. But they aren't "cookies." When the French say "coo-kee"—the accent approximating that of the Cookie Monster on *Sesame Street*—they mean only one kind: chocolate chip. The French are nuts about chocolate-chip cookies. One popular brand has a label that depicts a Texas longhorn and a likeness of Wyatt Earp. What longhorns and Wyatt Earp have to do with chocolate-chip cookies eludes me, but the French are also wild about the American West. So apparently this is a logical association to a Frenchman and no doubt a coup of marketing genius.

Pat Paquette, "The 'Coo-kee' Is Made with Chocolate Chips,"
Smithsonian, December 1999: 132.

23.4 Paragraph Division

■ *Divide the following passage into paragraphs by inserting the sign ¶. The original passage contains three paragraphs.*

American mythology makes common cause with another formidable force: American complacency. Harold Stevenson's work in 1979–1980 with children, mothers, and teachers from three countries suggests the problem by contrasting performance and attitudes. In one statistical exercise he rated the mathematics achievement of equal numbers of students from Japan, Taiwan, and the United States. Among the top 100 first-graders there were only fifteen American children. Almost unbelievably, among the top 100 fifth-graders there was only one American child. In contrast, among the bottom 100 first-graders, fifty-eight were American, and among the bottom 100 fifth-graders, sixty-seven were American. There was more. The shocker came in the attitude surveys. More than 40 percent of the American mothers were "very satisfied" with how their children were doing in school, whereas less than 5 percent of the Japanese and Chinese mothers were "very satisfied." Nearly a third of the Chinese and Japanese mothers said they were "not satisfied" with their children's performance, but only 10 percent of the American mothers expressed dissatisfaction. The jarring enthusiasm of the Americans persisted when it came to attitudes toward the quality of the schools themselves. Ninety-one percent judged that the school was doing an "excellent" or a "good" job. Only 42 percent of the Chinese mothers and 39 percent of the Japanese mothers were this positive.

Michael J. Barrett, "The Case for More School Days,"
The Atlantic, November 1990: 94.

23.5 Digressive Sentences

■ *In the blank at the bottom of each paragraph, write the number of any sentence that is digressive. Any paragraph may contain as many as three such sentences.*

EXAMPLE

(1) To use a library efficiently, one must first learn how books are classified in the computerized catalog. (2) These catalogs are located usually on a library's main floor—but not always. (3) Books are listed in three ways: by author, by title, and by subject. (4) Thus if one knows a title, but not an author or a subject, one can easily locate a book.

_____

A. (1) Every year thousands of Americans fly across the country with their pets. (2) With a little forethought, these owners can reduce the stress their favorite animal will experience in flight. (3) The best way to transport smaller pets is in a cage designed to fit beneath a plane seat. (4) Fellow travelers may be allergic to animal hair and dander. (5) Larger pets will have to travel in the cargo section. (6) An article of clothing permeated with the owner's scent can help calm them in this unfamiliar setting.

_____

B. (1) Financial aid for students includes basic grants, work-study jobs, scholarships, and loans. (2) In the past, students who required financial assistance often had to drop out of school and work for a few months. (3) Many students simultaneously receive aid from several of these sources, usually combining scholarships with work-study programs. (4) College administrations continually solicit alumni for more money. (5) Jobs are especially popular because they may provide valuable experience for a future vocation. (6) Some of the country's most distinguished citizens received scholarships. (7) All students in need of financial assistance qualify for aid in one form or another. (8) Even if they must borrow from university loan funds, they usually pay only minimal interest charges. (9) Students who desire assistance should contact their school's financial aid office for additional information.

_____

C. (1) Marathon swimmers are a distinct breed. (2) Unlike most athletes, they are stocky rather than lithe. (3) Relatively large amounts of body fat help them float as well as insulate them from frigid water. (4) As their muscular physiques attest, Olympic-style swimmers train for bursts of speed. (5) Covering distances of one to sixty miles, marathon swimmers must be able to tolerate unusual amounts of physical pain and psychological stress. (6) In addition to nausea, jellyfish stings, and hypothermia, they must be able to endure prolonged exposure to salt water that can transform their faces into grotesque masks. (7) They must be able to shake off the hallucinations that tease or terrify them as they approach the limits of human endurance. (8) Needless to say, sheer doggedness is their strongest instinct.

_____

D. (1) To see the Grand Canyon as it should be seen, a visitor must rise before dawn. (2) The canyon is located in northern Arizona. (3) Just before the sun appears the walls of the canyon are a deep purple, and a visitor almost feels the eerie silence. (4) Gradually the canyon comes alive. (5) Soon there are the cries of a few birds. (6) Then with the first streaks of light, the rocks begin to glow in rich oranges and reds. (7) Finally, the details appear—the deep crevices, the patches of grass and mesquite and sage—and a visitor who looks closely may see a deer or chipmunk. (8) Later the visitor can visit the many shops located near Bright Angel Lodge and El Tovar.

_____

E. (1) The great cities before Rome (Corinth, Carthage, Syracuse) were trading and manufacturing centers. (2) Rome, on the other hand, was the financial and political capital of the Western world. (3) Rome never rivaled previous great cities in commerce or industry. (4) Another great city of the ancient world was Carthage, located in North Africa. (5) Rome usually imported most of its necessities and luxuries from cities and regions under its military and political control. (6) Sicily and Africa especially provided for Rome's agricultural needs such as corn. (7) During the so-called Golden Age of Greece, Athens was the intellectual center of Western civilization.

_____

F. (1) *El Niño*, the name given to warm currents that flow past the coasts of eastern South America, is a mixed blessing to the Western Hemisphere. (2) On the one hand, these currents bring rain to the arid coasts of Peru and Ecuador, and this usually barren region bursts into life with the arrival of badly needed moisture. (3) Further north, though, the same weather phenomenon brings floods that destroy crops, roads, bridges, and neighborhoods. (4) In addition, the southeastern United States is abnormally dry during these years. (5) These currents also coincide with droughts in parts of Australia and Southeast Asia.

_____

G. (1) The modern photographer needs more than a simple developing kit to process photographs at home. (2) Actually, developing them at home is probably more expensive than sending them to professional laboratories to develop them. (3) The most important and most expensive item required for film processing is a good enlarger. (4) If one develops negatives without an enlarger, the final pictures are almost too small to enjoy. (5) Used enlargers for sale are very difficult to find. (6) Furthermore, one should purchase an enlarging easel, an enlarger timer, and a focusing lens. (7) Only after buying this relatively expensive equipment can the amateur photographer hope to develop good-quality prints.

H. (1) In recent years, television weather coverage has taken on a new look. (2) No longer merely the subject of five-minute forecasts aired on local affiliates, weather now has its own cable channel and a new fascination for the viewing public. (3) Without a doubt, live broadcasts from every significant meteorological event, from hurricanes on the Atlantic coast to snowstorms in the Sierra Nevada, contribute to weather's new appeal. (4) Live-action reporting gives the weather a dramatic immediacy it lacked when traditional "weathermen" simply stood before colored maps of the nation. (5) Further, around-the-clock weather broadcasts on television have elevated some popular meteorologists to near-celebrity status. (6) By creating their own web sites, some of these new meteorologists have used the Internet to enhance their visibility.

I. (1) Archaeology is a much more exact science than many people realize. (2) For example, archaeologists have determined that on a day in late spring approximately 400,000 years ago, about twenty-five people made a brief visit to a cove on the Mediterranean coast near Nice, France. (3) From the study of fossil bones, stone tools, various imprints in the sand, and the density of the sand, scientists have reconstructed in detail much of the three-day sojourn. (4) Imprints give clues to where these ancient people slept and what they slept on. (5) Archaeology has really matured as a science and has become quite popular in the public's eye since Heinrich Schliemann's excavation of ancient cities in the late nineteenth century. (6) These imaginative scientists also know much about the food these nomadic people ate, how they prepared it, how they hunted for food, and how they protected the group from predators at night. (7) The human imagination simply has no limits.

J. (1) Every ten years, the Census Bureau undertakes the Herculean task of counting the estimated 275 million residents of the United States. (2) It begins by mailing questionnaires to every household. (3) It also blankets the nation with advertisements that explain how the census benefits communities. (4) For many reasons, however, a large percentage of the population never returns these forms. (5) Other countries are more successful in gathering similar data. (6) The next step is to send out thousands of temporary workers, who make personal calls and even interview neighbors in an effort to document as many residents as possible. (7) Despite these efforts, a large number of residents are never counted.

_____

K. (1) Public meetings between management and labor can be beneficial. (2) But one should not expect miracles. (3) Formal negotiations also may be detrimental if either side plays only to the press. (4) Informal contacts usually precede public meetings and set agendas. (5) This procedure often reduces the possibility of either side's grandstanding for publicity. (6) Indeed, these contacts usually are necessary for productive bargaining.

_____

L. (1) Successful interviewing for a job requires careful planning. (2) Some study of the prospective employer is necessary. (3) Factual knowledge about a firm or industry impresses personnel managers. (4) One should research the company or firm thoroughly in a library or through personal contacts with other employees. (5) The successful candidate knows the company's goals and makes them his or her own.

_____

M. (1) Not all cookies are good to eat. (2) Electronic "cookies"—identification numbers silently implanted in your computer when you visit certain web sites—threaten to make privacy a thing of the past. (3) Admittedly, cookies do have some benefits. (4) They remember your password when you return to a favorite site, and they are the technology that allows you to build a "shopping cart" when you buy items online. (5) As computer sales increase, so will the number of cookies. (6) Without careful restriction, though, cookies will let electronic businesses know, record, and even sell lists of every web site you have ever visited. (7) Worse yet, a record of your Internet habits could be used in the future by insurance companies, lawyers, or even personal enemies.

_____

N. (1) The American bald eagle seems to be making a comeback. (2) Once on the verge of extinction, the eagle now has increased its population throughout most of its range. (3) DDT pollution caused severe problems for the bald eagle. (4) It is now protected by law against hunters. (5) If not healthy, the bald eagle population has at least increased significantly.

_____

O. (1) Sunscreen and suntan lotions are modern inventions, designed for GIs stationed in the Pacific during World War II. (2) The enemy in the Pacific theater was Japan. (3) These lotions perhaps popularized the modern phenomenon of sunbathing, which, although popular, is in reality dangerous. (4) Until the 1920s, most Americans lived inland and rarely visited the beach. (5) With the ozone layer being depleted, the use of sunscreen lotion is vital. (6) Researchers have found that overexposure to the sun causes skin cancer in later life; therefore, a sunburn is more than a painful inconvenience—it is a health hazard.

_____

23.6 Sentence Functions

■ *Label the sentences in the following paragraph. Use* **T** *to identify the topic sentence,* **R** *to identify the restricting sentence(s), and* **S** *to identify supporting sentences.*

_____ It's not just in behavioral laboratories that animals display their cognitive powers, but also in the wild. _____ In fact, field biologists are finding that many species' natural behaviors are no less complex than the ones that psychologists are going to such lengths to teach them. _____ Research has shown, for example, that the calls of some free-ranging monkeys are not just raw expressions of arousal, as was long assumed, but fairly detailed news reports about events in the outside world. _____ Robert Syfarth and Dorothy Cheney of the University of Pennsylvania have found that vervet monkeys in Kenya have at least three distinct alarm calls—one for snakes, one for eagles, one for leopards—and that each one elicits a different response.

Geoffrey Cowley, "The Wisdom of Animals,"
Newsweek, 28 May 1988: 56–57.

DATE _____ SCORE _____

23.7 Sentence Functions

■ *Label the sentences in the following paragraph. Use **T** to identify the topic sentence,*
***R** to identify the restricting sentence(s), and **S** to identify supporting sentences.*

_____ The other emotional ingredients of conscience are that quaint pair, guilt and shame. _____ Although some child advocates insist that no child should ever be shamed, scientists who study moral development disagree. _____ "Guilt and shame are part of conscience," says Berkowitz. _____ In young children, the sense of right and wrong is born of the feeling that you have disappointed someone you love, usually your parents. _____ If there is no one whose love you need, whose disapproval breaks your heart, you are missing a crucial source of the emotions that add up to knowing right from wrong and acting on it.

Sharon Begley and Claudia Kalb, "Learning Right from Wrong,"
Newsweek, 13 March 2000: 31.

Copyright © by Houghton Mifflin Company. All rights reserved.

NAME _____

DATE _____ SCORE _____

23.8 Sentence Functions

■ *Label the sentences in the following paragraph. Use* **T** *to identify the topic sentence,* **R** *to identify the restricting sentence(s), and* **S** *to identify supporting sentences.*

_____ It was on the silver screen that the soda fountain truly reached stardom. _____ From the 1920s through the early '50s, the drugstore set was a Hollywood fixture. _____ D. W. Griffith was one of the first to explore the fountain's possibilities; in his 1919 charmer, *True Heart Suzie,* Lillian Gish is courted there weekly. _____ W. C. Fields' *It's the Old Army Game* (1926) is facetiously dedicated to the American druggist. _____ It was beside the fountain in 1938 that Mickey Rooney, as the quintessential teenager Andy Hardy, flirted with Judy Garland in *Love Finds Andy Hardy.* _____ With the box-office success of the Hardy series, the list of fountain-featuring films grew at a phenomenal pace.

David M. Schwartz, "Life Was Sweeter, and More Innocent, in Our Soda Days," *Smithsonian,* July 1986: 116.

NAME _____

DATE _____ SCORE _____

23.9 Sentence Functions

*Label the sentences in the following paragraph. Use **T** to identify the topic sentence, **R** to identify the restricting sentence(s), and **S** to identify supporting sentences.*

_____ The best-known sultan is probably Suleyman the Magnificent, who expanded the [Ottoman] bounds and came close to capturing Vienna in the sixteenth century. _____ History shows contrary sides of Suleyman. _____ A Venetian envoy described him as "by nature melancholy, much addicted to women, liberal, proud, hasty, and yet sometimes very gentle." _____ He wrote love poetry under the pen name Muhibbi and remained devoted for many years to a Ukranian concubine named Roxelana, whom he married. _____ In one poem, he describes Roxelana, who took the name Hurrem after her conversion to Islam, as "My sheer delight, my revelry, my feast, my torch, my sunshine, my sun in heaven;/ My orange, my pomegranate, the flaming candle that lights up my pavilion." _____ Often called the Lawgiver, Suleyman codified and simplified a complex and confusing array of legal procedures. _____ His code attempted to wipe out discriminatory practices against Christian subjects and eased the draconian punishments against criminals.

Stanley Meisler, "Splendors of Topkapi," *Smithsonian,* February 2000: 121.

24 Paragraph Development

The kind of support offered in a paragraph, as well as the order in which it is presented, depends on the paragraph's purpose. Most paragraphs fall into one of the categories listed below.

OPENING AND CLOSING PARAGRAPHS

An opening paragraph can have several functions. First, it must present enough background explanation to help the reader see the context, the relevance, and the importance of the discussion. The paragraph might also entice its reader to continue reading by presenting an eye-catching fact, description, example, or assertion. Finally, it must present the main idea or thesis and thus orient the reader to the discussion that follows. In opening paragraphs, the background and interest-creating material generally precede the thesis statement. Notice how the following paragraph introduces a discussion of a trend in aircraft design.

> With their swept-back wings, forward-mounted canards, or stabilizers, and pusher propellers, they look a little as if they should be moving through the air tailfirst. But the two new designs—Beech Aircraft's Starship and Rinaldo Piaggio's P. 180 Avanti—are very much forward-looking pieces of machinery. Using advanced technology to deliver high performance and good fuel efficiency, they could dictate the shape of small transport aircraft in the coming years.
>
> Philip Elmer-Dewitt, "The Shape of Planes to Come,"
> *Time,* 27 June 1988: 65.

Closing paragraphs also have several functions. They may reassert the general relevance of the discussion, explore its ramifications, or concede its limitations. If the discussion has been long or complicated, the closing paragraph may reiterate the essay's major points. Elmer-Dewitt closes his article on new airplane designs by recognizing potential marketing difficulties. He quotes Henry Ogrodzinski, the communications director of the General Aviation Manufacturers Association, whom he introduced in an earlier paragraph.

> How much the demand will benefit the Starship and the Avanti is uncertain. The manufacturers still have to demonstrate that their performance claims are valid. Moreover, some executives may not like the idea of entrusting their lives to such novel and unusual designs. Ogrodzinski, for one, thinks they will. "Looks and status have always been a selling point in corporate aircraft," he says. "There is a certain prestige in owning the latest design."

PARAGRAPHS OF DESCRIPTION

Descriptive paragraphs help the reader envision a person or group of people, a place, an object, or an event. These paragraphs are usually developed by details that answer such common questions as who, what, when, where, why, and how about the subject. At other times they are developed by details that appeal to the reader's senses of hearing, sight, touch, and even smell and taste. The details in these paragraphs are usually organized by time or place. Garrison Keillor's description below, for example, is organized by place, moving from near to far as he first describes a house, then the barnyard behind it, then the fields beyond.

> In 1970, . . . I moved out to a farmhouse on the rolling prairie in central Minnesota, near Freeport, where I planted a garden and wrote stories to support my wife and year-old son. Rent was $80 a month. It got us a big square brick house with a porch that looked out on a peaceful barnyard, a granary and machine sheds and corncribs and silo, and the barn and feedlot where Norbert, the farmer whom I rented from, kept his beef cattle. Beyond the windbreak of red oak and spruce to the west and north lay a hundred sixty acres of his corn and oats. . . . Our long two-rut driveway ran due north through the woods to where the gravel road made an L, where our mailbox stood, where you could stand and see for a couple miles in all directions. . . .
>
> Garrison Keillor, "Laying on Our Backs Looking Up at the Stars,"
> *Newsweek,* 4 July 1988: 32.

PARAGRAPHS OF DEFINITION

Whereas descriptive paragraphs help readers understand concrete subjects, paragraphs of definition help them understand abstract ones. Usually paragraphs of definition clarify the meaning of ideas; special, unusual, or technical terms, or even proposals. These paragraphs typically begin by identifying and describing their subject's distinguishing characteristics and by presenting examples. To convey a clear, complete, and balanced impression, a defining paragraph might also include points about what the subject is *not*.

> To my biased taste, Cantonese cuisine is the greatest of all the Chinese cookery. The classical Cantonese style emphasizes freshness of ingredients and subtle but distinct contrasts of tastes and textures. A single dish is often composed of sweet and sour flavors, crispy and creamy or crunchy and tender textures and hot and cold temperatures. Gentle, quick cooking preserves the delicate natural flavors, colors and aromas of this fresh food. Soy, hoisin and oyster sauces—all relatively mild and congenial—are its mainstays. There is not an overdose of garlic, sharp spices and heavy oils. It is definitely not greasy.
>
> Ken Hom, "The Road to Canton,"
> *The New York Times Magazine,* 5 June 1988: 57.

In this paragraph, Ken Hom defines Cantonese cuisine first by describing its general characteristics, then by identifying its typical ingredients. As the paragraph concludes, he distinguishes its flavors from those characteristic of other types of food.

PARAGRAPHS OF COMPARISON AND CONTRAST

Paragraphs may offer literal comparisons of persons, places, proposals, objects, or ideas, or they may offer figurative comparisons, called **analogies.** Paragraphs may also identify the differences between two things that appear similar. Such paragraphs of comparison and contrast usually identify specific points of similarity or dissimilarity between the two things being compared. Any of the points used to describe or define may be used as features to compare or contrast. The following paragraph, for example, contrasts the positive and negative factors affecting the marketability of commercially raised venison in New Zealand.

> Deer have some advantages over cattle and sheep as food. Venison is lean, about 10 percent fat compared to more than 20 percent for lamb or beef. Thus it appeals to today's calorie-conscious markets. It is, however, more expensive—farm prices are almost $6 per kilogram in New Zealand compared to $1.60 for beef or $.70 for lamb.
>
> T. H. Clutton-Brock, "Red Deer and Man,"
> *National Geographic,* October 1986: 550.

PARAGRAPHS OF ANALYSIS

Analytical paragraphs divide a large group of ideas, events, objects, or people into parts. These paragraphs can take several forms.

Paragraphs that analyze through **classification and division** show the way in which a single item or a group of items can be logically divided into discrete parts. In these paragraphs, each subcategory is briefly defined, and the subcategories may be compared or contrasted with each other. In the following paragraph, Thomas Pyles classifies American regional dialects by the places in which they occur.

> In American English there are three main regional types—Northern, Midland, and Southern—with a good many different blendings of these as one travels westward. . . . There are also a number of subtypes on the Atlantic Coast, such as the speech of the New York and Boston areas in the North and the Charleston-Savannah area in the South. All types of American English have grown out of the regional modifications of the British Standard—with some coloring from the British dialects—as it existed in the seventeenth century, when it was much less rigid than it is today.
>
> Thomas Pyles, *The Origins and Development of the English Language,*
> 2nd ed. (New York: Harcourt, 1971), 235.

Paragraphs that analyze **cause and effect** show how past events or situations affect events or situations that follow them or how present situations or events may affect the future. These paragraphs list several causes or effects or explain a single one. The following paragraph presents some projected long-term effects from a change in the earth's atmosphere.

With a diminished ozone layer, more UV [ultraviolet radiation] from the sun will reach the earth. Scientists believe that more UV will induce mutations in the organisms that anchor the food chain of the world's oceans. UV threatens not only to cause more cases of skin cancer but also to damage the immune system, a blow that could leave us defenseless against infectious diseases. More UV may damage crops worth billions of dollars. "It is no exaggeration to say that the health and safety of millions of people around the world are at stake," says David Doniger of the Natural Resources Defense Council.

Sharon Begley, "A Gaping Hole in the Sky,"
Newsweek, 11 July 1988: 21.

Paragraphs that analyze **process** divide an action into a series of steps. These paragraphs identify, then describe or define, each step involved. They are always arranged from first to last in strictly chronological order. Notice how the following paragraph specifies the steps involved in successfully planting one species of grape.

For a maximum fruit production, use a wire trellis; it provides the best support for muscadines. To build a trellis, first drive a 4- to 5-foot stake into the ground beside the vine at planting time. Then, when the vine starts growing, select the strongest shoot to become the main stem and tie it to the stake. During the first summer, remove all side shoots. When the stem reaches the top of the stake, pinch off its tip to encourage growth of side shoots.

Steve Bender, "The Not-So-Lowly Muscadine,"
Progressive Farmer, July 1988: 59.

PARAGRAPHS OF ASSERTION

Perhaps the most common type of paragraph supports a statement of belief, an assertion of value, a judgment, or a generalization. These paragraphs are usually supported by facts, examples, statistics, statements by authorities, or eyewitness accounts. The paragraph below uses historical facts to support its assertion about Olympic Games of the past.

In fact, the Games of the Greeks were just as flawed as our own. It was the Greek tyrant Pheidon of Argos who seized Olympia in the seventh century B.C. for the glorification of his strong-arm regime. Two neighboring city-states, Elis and Pisa, fought for generations over the right to control the Games and collect their revenues. Sometimes such conflicts ended in an "An-Olympiad" or non-Olympics: the Games did not always go on.

Frank Holt, "An Olympic-Size Delusion,"
Newsweek, 16 July 1984: 16.

24.1 Paragraph Development

■ *Identify the type of development (description, definition, comparison and contrast, classification/division analysis, cause-and-effect analysis, process analysis, or assertion with support) used in each of the following paragraphs.*

1. Even the kindest and most well-intentioned parent will sometimes become exasperated. The difference between the good and the not-so-good parent in such situations is that the good parent will realize that his exasperation probably has more to do with himself than with what the child did, and that showing his exasperation will not be to anyone's advantage. The not-so-good parent, in contrast, believes that his exasperation was caused only by his child and that therefore he has every right to act on it.

    Bruno Bettelheim, "Punishment versus Discipline,"
    The Atlantic, November 1985: 52.

    Method of development: _____

2. The data raise haunting questions. If warming continues, how will melting permafrost transform landscapes? Will forests grow instead of tundra? Will wetlands rise where forests once grew? And will these changes affect the carbon balance, as the now unfrozen soil emits greater quantities of carbon dioxide (CO_2), a greenhouse gas that traps heat in the atmosphere?

    Bernice Wuethrich, "When Permafrost Isn't," *Smithsonian*, February 2000: 31–32.

    Method of development: _____

3. The male eagle is a model husband for these times. He does his share of home building by gathering sticks—often six feet long—for the base of the nest. Barreling into the desired branch at full speed, he hits it with his feet, grabs it with his talons as it cracks and flies away with it. He takes his turn sitting on the nest and helps feed and care for the newborns. According to Hodges's current study, one of the parents remains at the nest constantly until the eaglets are four weeks old.

    Sharon Begley, "Comeback for a National Symbol,"
    Newsweek, 9 July 1984: 65.

    Method of development: _____

4. Amid five acres of paddocks, pens, and fields stands a sturdy roundhouse, more than forty feet in diameter and thirty feet high, its basketwork walls plastered with daub. The thatched, conical roof, where swallows nest, protects ovens and querns and crockery. Immediately outside are several haystacks and a byre. A low bank and a shallow dike enclose the central compound. Beyond lie fields of wheat, barley, beans, and flax. In outlying pastures livestock graze—unusual breeds of sheep and cattle, gamey and hirsute.

Cullen Murphy, "The Buster Experiment,"
The Atlantic, August 1985: 20.

Method of development: _____

5. The plain fact is that American history is not intelligible, and we are not intelligible to ourselves, without a firm grasp of the life and ideas of the ancient world, of Judaism and Christendom in the Middle Ages, of feudalism, of the Renaissance and the Reformation, of the English Revolution and Enlightenment. The first settlers did not sail into view out of a void, their minds blank as the Atlantic Ocean. They were shaped and scarred by tens of centuries of religious, social, literary, and political experience. Their notions of honor and heroism were learned from Greco-Roman myth and history, from the Bible and the lives of the saints of the church, from stories of knights and crusaders, explorers and sea dogs of the Renaissance, soldiers and martyrs of the wars of religion. Those who sailed west to America came in fact not to build a New World but to bring to life in a new setting what they treasured most from the Old World.

Paul Gagnon, "Why Study History?"
The Atlantic, November 1988: 46–47.

Method of development: _____

24.2 Paragraph Development

■ *Identify the type of development (description, definition, comparison and contrast, classification/division analysis, cause-and-effect analysis, process analysis, or assertion with support) used in each of the following paragraphs.*

1. One good way to knead is to push hard into the dough with both heels of your hands and then pull the top edge toward you so that it looks like the crest of a wave. When the dough is too stiff to be stirred, it's ready to be kneaded. Cover a flat surface and your hands with flour, keeping track of how much you use by taking it from the remaining cup or so. Knead more flour in by tablespoons, adding it as the white powder disappears.

   Corby Kummer, "Parlor Pizza,"
   The Atlantic, April 1985: 129.

   Method of development: _____

2. As strange as it may seem, modern biochemistry has shown that the cell is operated by machines—literally, molecular machines. Like their man-made counterparts (such as mousetraps, bicycles, and space shuttles), molecular machines range from the simple to the enormously complex: mechanical, force-generating machines, like those in muscles; electronic machines, like those in nerves; and solar-powered machines, like those of photosynthesis. Of course, molecular machines are made primarily of proteins, not metal and plastic. In this chapter I will discuss molecular machines that allow cells to swim, and you will see what is required for them to do so.

   Michael J. Behe, *Darwin's Black Box* (New York: Touchstone, 1996) p. 51.

   Method of development: _____

3. I see several advantages to reintegrating grammar into the writing curriculum under this new conception of its role. First, teachers have an incentive to teach it more frequently and with more enthusiasm. Second, the public can take heart that we are getting "back to basics" at last. As always, of course, some people will not learn even the handbook rules; some will learn those and nothing more; and some will find the handbook rules a help in learning the real grammar of the written language. Perhaps more students will learn to write grammatical prose, but that is

less important than that more students may discover what it means to write well.

Geoffrey Nunberg, "An Apology for Grammar," *National Forum,* Fall 1985: 15.

Method of development: _____

4. What in any language is regarded as the "same sound" is actually a group of similar sounds which make up what is known as a phoneme. A phoneme is thus the smallest *distinctive* unit of speech: it consists of a number of allophones, that is, of similar sounds which are not distinctive. Thus, speakers of English regard as the "same sound" the sound spelled *t* in tone and stone, though actually a different sound is symbolized by the letter *t* in each of these words. . . .

Thomas Pyles, *The Origins and Development of the English Language,* 2nd ed. (New York: Harcourt, 1971), p. 30.

Method of development: _____

5. College will always convey a certain image: Gothic buildings filled with postadolescents listening to tweed-clad professors. But the Internet is blurring that picture, and State U is quietly morphing into College.com. To be sure, a virtual university is no place for Felicity or her just-out-of-high-school friends; they want the full campus package, kegs and all. But "typical" college students—18–22 years old, living in dorms, studying full time—make up only 16 percent of enrollment today, says Arthur Levine, president of Teachers College at Columbia University. They're far outnumbered by the 79 percent of adults who lack diplomas. Many of these folks have kids, work irregular hours or travel, which makes night school impossible. The result: millions of adults are dialing for diplomas. They're attending start-up schools you've never hear of—and prestigious ones like Columbia, Stanford, and Duke. By the end of the year, according to researchers at InterEd, 75 percent of all U.S. universities will offer online course work, and 5.8 million students will have logged on. Study anytime! College has never been more convenient.

Daniel McGinn, "College Online," *Newsweek,* 24 April 2000: 56.

Method of development: _____

25 Paragraph Transitions

Paragraphs are easier for readers to follow when the connections between the various words and ideas are easy to detect. To clarify those connections, use an effective array of transitional devices.

TRANSITIONAL DEVICES

Effective writers use various elements of style to help clarify and explain the relationships between sentences. Transitional words and phrases, reference words, repeated words, and repeated sentence patterns are all ways to show these relationships.

Transitional words and phrases can indicate time and place (*before, while, during, when, where*), addition (*and, furthermore, in fact*), contrast (*but, however, although, on the other hand*), or causation (*so, therefore, consequently, because*).

Reference words include personal pronouns (*her, he, hers, his, its, their, they*), demonstrative adjectives (*this, those, these, that*), and comparatives (*more, less, greater, fewer*).

Repeated words include not only the same words but also synonyms and general terms of class that include words used earlier. In the following sentence, *students* is a class term referring back to the more specific word *freshmen*.

> Many freshmen find registration bewildering. These students quickly learn ways to make the process more tolerable.

In the following passage, transitional words and phrases are underlined once, reference words are underlined twice, and repeated words or variations on the same word are circled.

Throughout, the original intention of scholarship persists, whether duly or poorly carried out: it is analysis—that is, the narrow scrutiny of an object for the purpose of drawing conclusions. These in turn must be supported by original arguments and must take into account the previous arguments of others, known as "the literature" of the subject. It is clear that as the analysts multiply and the literature accumulates, the subject that anyone is able to deal with grows smaller. In other words, specialization is unavoidable; and thus it is that specialism, <u>which</u> is a state of mind, follows (specialization) <u>which</u> is a practi-

cal necessity.

Jacques Barzun, "Scholarship Versus Culture,"
The Atlantic, November 1984: 99.

Repeated sentence structure helps to clarify sentence relationships. Often sentences that present parallel reasons or explanations do so in grammatically parallel ways. Sentences at different levels of specificity should not be grammatically parallel, however. Notice how repeated structure helps tie together the sentences in the following paragraph. Repeated structures are underlined twice.

Yet <u>punctuation is something more</u> than a culture's birthmark; <u>it scores the music</u> in our minds, gets our thoughts moving to the rhythm of our hearts. <u>Punctuation is the notation</u> in the sheet music of our words, telling us when to rest, or when to raise our voices; <u>it acknowledges</u> that the meaning of our discourse, as of any symphonic composition, lies not in the units but in the pauses, the pacing and the phrasing. <u>Punctuation is the way</u> one bats one's eyes, lowers one's voice, or blushes demurely. <u>Punctuation adjusts</u> the tone and color and volume till the feeling comes into perfect focus.

Pico Iyer, "In Praise of the Humble Comma,"
Time, 13 June 1988: 80.

25.1 Transitions

- *Circle the transitional words and phrases, including coordinating conjunctions, subordinating conjunctions, and conjunctive adverbs.*

All moose are of a single circumpolar species, *Alces alces,* found in most

of Canada, northern Russia, a corner of Poland and parts of Scandinavia, as

well as Alaska and the previously mentioned states. In Sweden, moose are

so plentiful in some areas that they pose a serious traffic hazard. The same

is true in parts of Alaska. On the Kenai Peninsula, as many as 250 moose

have been killed on the highways in one year. But although a one-ton car can

readily triumph over a half-ton moose, it's a Pyrrhic victory. As one Alaskan

wildlife biologist puts it: "You've seen the damage an ordinary white-tailed

deer can do to a car? You should see what a bull moose can do!"

John Madson, "The North Woods: A Horn of Plenty for Old Bucketnose,"
Smithsonian, July 1986: 104.

25.2 Transitions

- *Circle the reference words, including personal pronouns and demonstrative adjectives.*

Chaplin's impact was so strong and swift that within months of his screen debut he was one of the movies' biggest stars. By the end of the first year in films he was, without exaggeration, the most famous man in the world. It didn't take a high-priced media campaign to orchestrate his success; the public made him a star. It was said that all a theater manager had to do to guarantee a crowd was to place in front of his box office a cardboard cutout of the Tramp bearing the slogan "He's Here Today!" He inspired toys, dolls, comic strips, popular songs, highbrow articles, lowbrow imitators, and unprecedented adulation—all of this before TV or radio to help spread the word. Even today, a major computer company, IBM, has chosen the Tramp to represent Everyman who struggles to survive in the high-tech '80's.

Leonard Matlin, "Silent-Film Buffs Stalk and Find a Missing Tramp,"
Smithsonian, July 1986: 46–47.

25.3 Transitions

■ *Circle the repeated words, including same words, synonyms, and terms of class.*

She has a thousand names and faces—and countless tasks and talents. Even as a fierce warrior heroically slaying the most vicious demons, she retains her composure and radiant beauty. Westerners accustomed to a "Heavenly Father," and to seeing virginal, subdued images of the Madonna, might find Devi and her wildly vigorous feminine power quite startling.

For many Hindus, however, Devi's greatest strength is that she embodies *all* aspects of womanhood. In the vast pantheon, she is in the top tier, as powerful as the male gods Vishnu and Shiva. Mother goddess of India and local protector for innumerable villages, she can be quiet and nurturing. But she is also a cosmic force, addressing the creation and destruction of worlds. On occasion she is voluptuous and alluring—a playful temptress, a passionate lover. Before exams, Hindu pupils pray to her, incarnated as Sarasvati, the goddess of music and learning. Devi blesses her devotees with fortune and success.

Bruce Hathaway, "The Great Goddess Devi," *Smithsonian*, June 1999: 115.

NAME _____

DATE _____ SCORE _____

25.4 Transitions

■ *Underline repeated sentence patterns.*

Good reading, therefore, though it is not essentially an affectional or moral or intellectual activity, has something in common with all three. In love we escape from our self into one another. In the moral sphere, every act of justice or charity involves putting ourselves in the other person's place and thus transcending our own competitive particularity. In coming to understand anything, we are rejecting the facts as they are for us in favour of the facts as they are. The primary impulse of each is to maintain and aggrandise himself. The secondary impulse is to go out of the self, to correct its provincialism and heal its loneliness. In love, in virtue, in the pursuit of the arts, we are doing this.

C. S. Lewis, *An Experiment in Criticism* (London: Cambridge U P, 1961), p. 138.

Cross-References to
Practical English Handbook, ELEVENTH EDITION